FLOYD CLYMER'S MOTORCYCLIST'S LIBRARY

The Book of the
PANTHER (H/WT)

A PRACTICAL GUIDE TO THE HANDLING AND
MAINTENANCE OF THE 1938-63 598 C.C. MODEL 100
AND THE 1959-66 645 C.C. MODEL 120 P. & M. PANTHERS

BY

W. C. HAYCRAFT
F.R.S.A.

THIRD EDITION

1967

ANNOUNCEMENT

By special arrangement with the original publishers of this book, Sir Isaac Pitman & Son, Ltd., of London, England, we have secured the exclusive publishing rights for this book, as well as all others in THE MOTORCYCLIST'S LIBRARY.

Included in THE MOTORCYCLIST'S LIBRARY are complete instruction manuals covering the care and operation of respective motorcycles and engines; valuable data on speed tuning, and thrilling accounts of motorcycle race events. See listing of available titles elsewhere in this edition.

We consider it a privilege to be able to offer so many fine titles to our customers.

FLOYD CLYMER
Publisher of Books Pertaining to Automobiles and Motorcycles

2125 W. PICO ST.   LOS ANGELES 6, CALIF.

INTRODUCTION

Welcome to the world of digital publishing ~ the book you now hold in your hand, while unchanged from the original edition, was printed using the latest state of the art digital technology. The advent of print-on-demand has forever changed the publishing process, never has information been so accessible and it is our hope that this book serves your informational needs for years to come. If this is your first exposure to digital publishing, we hope that you are pleased with the results. Many more titles of interest to the classic automobile and motorcycle enthusiast, collector and restorer are available via our website at www.VelocePress.com. We hope that you find this title as interesting as we do.

NOTE FROM THE PUBLISHER

The information presented is true and complete to the best of our knowledge. All recommendations are made without any guarantees on the part of the author or the publisher, who also disclaim all liability incurred with the use of this information.

TRADEMARKS

We recognize that some words, model names and designations, for example, mentioned herein are the property of the trademark holder. We use them for identification purposes only. This is not an official publication.

INFORMATION ON THE USE OF THIS PUBLICATION

This manual is an invaluable resource for the classic motorcycle enthusiast and a "must have" for owners interested in performing their own maintenance. However, in today's information age we are constantly subject to changes in common practice, new technology, availability of improved materials and increased awareness of chemical toxicity. As such, it is advised that the user consult with an experienced professional prior to undertaking any procedure described herein. While every care has been taken to ensure correctness of information, it is obviously not possible to guarantee complete freedom from errors or omissions or to accept liability arising from such errors or omissions. Therefore, any individual that uses the information contained within, or elects to perform or participate in do-it-yourself repairs or modifications acknowledges that there is a risk factor involved and that the publisher or its associates cannot be held responsible for personal injury or property damage resulting from the use of the information or the outcome of such procedures.

WARNING!

One final word of advice, this publication is intended to be used as a reference guide, and when in doubt the reader should consult with a qualified technician.

PREFACE

HEAVYWEIGHT P. & M. Model 100 Panthers with their powerful sloping push-rod type 598 c.c. O.H.V. engines incorporating the best features of modern engine design have been manufactured for years by Phelon & Moore Ltd., and need no introduction.

Because of their striking appearance, precision finish, robustness, surging power, reliability, and economical running, Model 100 Panthers steadily increased in popularity, especially among sidecar riders. In 1959 the attractive and extremely powerful Model 120 was introduced. Similar to Model 100 except for engine capacity and some minor details, it proved so popular among sidecar enthusiasts that in 1963 the production of the smaller capacity Model 100 ceased and since then factory production has been concentrated on Model 120 and a fine sidecar chassis for fitting to it.

For heavy-duty sidecar work the 645 c.c. Model 120 Panther is generally recognized to be in every respect an ideal mount. It is possible to fit readily almost any proprietary make of sidecar, and with one or more passengers the outfit will romp up the worst of gradients in an effortless manner. Full details of this reasonably priced model (with or without sidecar) can be obtained by contacting George Clarke (Motors) Ltd. of 276-278 Brixton Hill, London, S.W.2 or Phelon & Moore Ltd., P.O. Box 14, Cleckheaton, Yorkshire.

The purpose of this handbook is to help you, if you have already bought a new or second-hand Model 100 or 120 Panther, to obtain the maximum pleasure, mileage, m.p.g., m.p.h., and m.p.£.

As far as possible the author has avoided purely descriptive matter and has devoted most of the available space to the practical maintenance of rigid and spring-frame Panthers.

The present edition covers fully all 1938-66 598, 645 c.c. Models 100 and 120 Panthers. Where the paragraph headings are not dated, the subject matter applies to *all* these models.

In conclusion, I am very grateful to Phelon & Moore Ltd., for assistance in regard to technical data and for permitting some illustrations to be reproduced; to the firm's Technical Dept. for kindly reading the proofs, and to the makers of various accessories for their helpful co-operation.

W. C. H.

CONTENTS

CHAP.		PAGE
	PREFACE	
I.	HANDLING A PANTHER	1
II.	THE AMAL CARBURETTOR	17
III.	CORRECT LUBRICATION	27
IV.	MAINTAINING A GOOD SPARK	44
V.	THE LIGHTING SET	58
VI.	GENERAL MAINTENANCE	79
	INDEX	137

CHAPTER I

HANDLING A PANTHER

THIS chapter is mainly for the benefit of those who have never before handled a heavyweight Panther and perhaps have had little or no previous motor-cycling experience. The handling of a Panther is quickly mastered, the engine being very responsive, and all controls conveniently located and easy to operate. Some useful advice is given on starting up, gear changing, sidecar driving, running-in, etc.

Insurance, Licences, etc. Note that you are not permitted to ride *any* type of motor-cycle on the public highway if you are under 16 years of age. Also note the following points to avoid coming into conflict with the Law—

1. You are legally obliged to take out insurance to cover all *third-party* risks. Make sure that you obtain the vitally important "Certificate of Insurance." If you have bought a new Panther you cannot obtain this certificate until the machine has been registered and a registration number allocated to it. When a machine is bought on hire-purchase terms full comprehensive insurance is generally required. Such insurance is recommended also for all new machines bought outright.

2. Obtain a registration book and registration licence. If your machine is new or has changed hands, fill up Form R.F.1/2. To renew a registration licence, fill up Form R.F.1/A. On Form R.F.1/2 you are required to state the engine and frame numbers. These are located on the near-side of the oil sump and the off-side of the frame below the dualseat respectively. The registration licence must be in a waterproof holder facing the near-side. All Model 100 and Model 120 Panthers are taxed at £8 per annum whether ridden solo or with a sidecar attached.

3. Obtain a "provisional" (six months) driving licence if you are a novice and have not passed a driving test. It can be renewed as required and the application form for each licence is Form D.L.1. Each licence costs 10s. Note that a "learner" must not ride a motor-cycle having a capacity exceeding 250 c.c. You cannot therefore learn to ride on a heavyweight Panther. While having only a "provisional" licence you must also not carry a pillion passenger unless he or she holds a current "full" driving licence. Immediately you get a driving licence sign it in ink.

4. If you hold only a "provisional" licence, mount "L" plates

at the front and rear of the machine and see that these do not obstruct the registration letters or numbers.

5. If you are a "learner" and feel capable of taking a driving test, the cost of which is £1, fill up Form D.L.26. After passing a driving test obtain a "full" (three year) driving licence which costs 15s. Form D.L.1 is the correct form for obtaining an initial "full" driving licence and for renewing it.

6. While riding always carry the driving licence and "Certificate

Fig. 1. Timing-side View of 1966 645 c.c. o.h.v. Spring-frame Panther Model 120

Basically of similar design to the well proved and popular 1938-63 598 c.c. Model 100, this very reliable, economical and attractive 598 c.c. Panther is the most powerful single-cylinder motor-cycle produced in the United Kingdom. It is an ideal mount for heavy duty solo and sidecar work.

of Insurance." Keep your registration book in a safe place and return it to the registration authorities for amendment if you change your address or sell the motor-cycle.

7. If you own an old or second-hand machine see that it is always in a roadworthy condition. Pay special attention to the brakes, tyres, steering, lights, horn, speedometer, etc. It is now an offence to ride a motor-cycle which is not in a roadworthy condition.

8. Make sure that your speedometer and rear number plate are easily read by night as well as by day. The speedometer must indicate within ± 10 per cent accuracy when 30 m.p.h. is being exceeded.

Some Sound Advice. All motor-cyclists, whether experienced or not, are strongly advised to—

1. Buy and read most carefully a copy of the 32-page booklet,

HANDLING A PANTHER

The Highway Code, and also a copy of the smaller booklet, *The New Traffic Signs*. Both are profusely illustrated, published by H.M. Stationery Office, and obtainable from most bookshops at 6d. each.

2. Wear a reliable crash helmet *always* while riding. This can prevent disastrous head injuries in the event of an accident. A crash helmet is quite cheap and is a really sound investment.

Vetting the Machine. If you have bought a new or second-hand model, scrutinize it carefully to make sure that all accessories and equipment are securely mounted, and with suitable spanners check over the various nuts for tightness, especially the external nuts on the engine and the engine supporting bolts. Switch on the headlamp and note whether the battery is properly charged. There should be no signs of dimming with the switch in the *H* position. Occasionally the h.t. lead from the magneto to the sparking-plug terminal becomes loose. Verify this small but vital point. Where a second-hand machine is concerned, it is always advisable to make a most thorough inspection before any attempt is made to get on the road, and indeed before buying the machine.

The Riding Position. It is essential to make sure right from the start that the riding position *is* the best obtainable, and that the various controls come readily and comfortably to hand. Where necessary, a combined adjustment should be made in respect of: (*a*) the angle of the handlebars, (*b*) the position of the footrests, (*c*) the position of the foot gear-change lever and (*d*) the angle of the control levers on the handlebars. The saddle or dualseat on the Panther is *not* adjustable.

(*a*) To adjust the handlebars for angle, slacken the four nuts on the clamping-bolts, and move the handlebars to the most convenient angle. Then see that the nuts are firmly retightened.

(*b*) To adjust the footrest position, loosen the nuts which hold the serrated faces of the footrest shafts and hangers in firm contact, and then move the footrest hangers to provide the most comfortable position for the feet. Retighten the nuts firmly.

(*c*) To adjust the position of the foot gear-change lever, remove the securing screw, which also retains the gear-change indicator pointer, and slacken the pinch-bolt; then alter the position of the lever on its splined shaft until gear changing can readily be effected with the minimum movement of the foot from the off-side footrest.

(*d*) To adjust the angle of the handlebar controls, so that the controls come readily to hand, loosen the clip-securing screws and then move the controls as required within the limits provided.

4   THE BOOK OF THE PANTHER HEAVYWEIGHT

The Model 100 or 120 Controls. Before attempting to start up, you should, if you have never before handled a Panther, get quite familiar with the layout of the controls and their operation. It is a good plan to sit on the saddle and "twiddle" the various

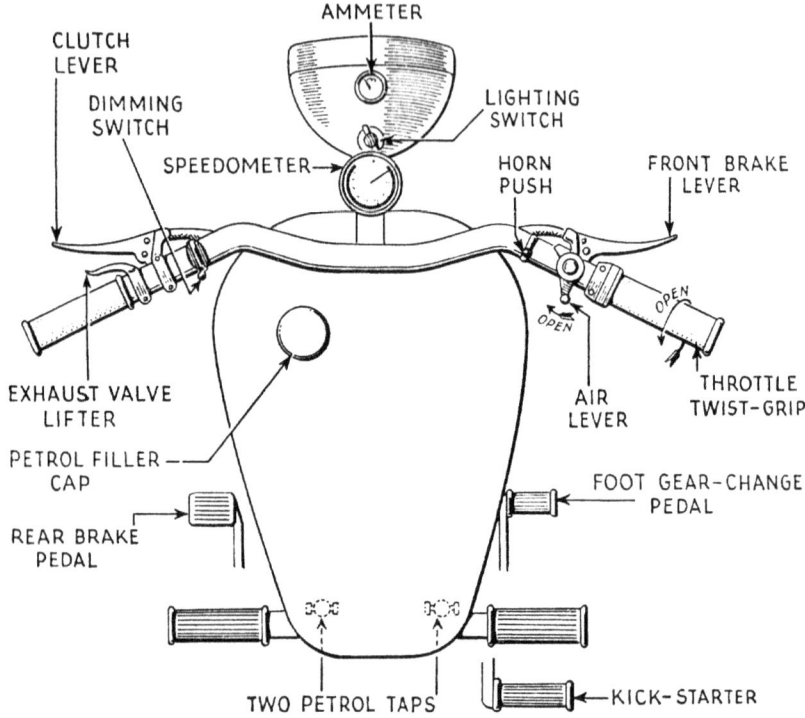

FIG. 2. THE PANTHER CONTROL LAYOUT (MODELS 100, 120)

The decompressor lever (see Fig. 3) is not shown. On 1938–46 and 1951–7 and later models (without automatic ignition-advance) an ignition lever is on the near side of the handlebars. All models have a steering damper (not shown). Speedometer is on headlamp for 1956–66.

levers while contemplating the effect it would have with the engine running.

The controls (see Fig. 2), mostly on the handlebars, may conveniently be divided into three groups: (1) engine controls, (2) cycle controls, and (3) electrical controls.

1. The engine controls consist of: (*a*) the throttle twist-grip, (*b*) the air lever, (*c*) the exhaust-valve lifter, and (*d*) the decompressor (or half-compression) lever. An ignition lever is provided on 1938–46 and 1951–66 models not fitted with automatic ignition-advance mechanism.

2. The cycle controls comprise; (*a*) the foot gear-change

pedal, (*b*) the clutch lever, (*c*) the front-brake lever, and (*d*) the rear-brake pedal.

3. The electrical controls are: (*a*) the lighting switch (see page 66), (*b*) the dimming switch, and (*c*) the horn push.

Inward Movement. Note that all handlebar controls are brought into positive operation by *inward* movement, i.e. towards the rider.

Concerning the Decompressor. The decompressor is mounted on the off side of the engine timing-case as shown in Fig. 3. It is brought into operation by moving the lever anti-clockwise (upwards) as far as it will go. To enable the decompressor to be moved fully, it is necessary to raise the valve lifter temporarily.

Note that with the decompressor in use, the engine continues to perform the normal four-stroke cycle of operations. The Panther decompressor releases *a portion of the mixture* during the *compression* stroke only, and facilitates easy starting of a 598 c.c. or 645 c.c. engine with a 6·5 to 1 compression ratio.

STARTING UP ENGINE

Verify that the inflation pressures of the front, rear, and sidecar (if fitted) tyres are correct (see page 115) and then attend to fuel and oil replenishment. Open the quickly-detachable hinged filler cap and from a pump, or can and funnel, fill the tank (empty on a new machine) which has a capacity of 3 gal. (4 gal., 1953 onwards).

As regards oil replenishment, suitable brands and grades of engine oils are given on page 32. Withdraw the combined filler cap and dip-stick situated low down on the off side of the crank-case and replenish with suitable engine oil to the correct level (top notch for a new machine).

The capacity of the oil-sump reservoir is four pints, and on a new machine (except export models) the reservoir is filled with approximately this amount of engine oil. After the initial filling, check the oil level regularly and keep it high (see page 43).

Adjusting Controls for Starting. Setting the controls for quick and easy starting is a knack which is quickly mastered. For starting up (cold), the normal control setting is as follows—

1. First verify that the foot gear-change lever is in the *neutral* (*N*) position (see Fig. 4), as shown by the indicator attached to the shaft. The rear wheel should, of course, rotate freely, with the machine on its stand.

2. Open *one* of the twin petrol taps provided. Keep the other tap shut so as to maintain a reserve fuel supply in the petrol tank. For starting up and all normal running, it is preferable to use the

near-side petrol tap. This enables you to see the actual amount of petrol available before switching over to the reserve supply. If the off-side petrol tap is turned to the "On" position, you will see through the filler cap orifice only the amount of petrol held in reserve, and be badly misguided.

3. Open the throttle twist-grip (anti-clockwise movement) very slightly—about one-eighth.

4. Close the air lever completely, unless the engine is already warmed up, in which case open it fully.

5. On 1938-46, late 1950 and later models, set the ignition lever in the three-quarter full-advance (inwards) position. On 1947 to early 1950 models with Lucas automatic ignition-advance, an ignition lever is omitted.

6. Flood the carburettor slightly by depressing the tickler on top of the float chamber, keeping it depressed for a few seconds. If the engine has already been warmed up, flooding should *not* be attempted. Flood the carburettor so that petrol just starts to drip from its base.

Starting Up (Engine Cold). If a stiff engine, particularly a new one, is to be started up from cold in wintry conditions, it is desirable to free the slipper-type piston by breaking down the congealed oil film (see that winter-grade oil is used) before attempting to start. To free the piston, set the controls as described on page 5. Next, with the kick-starter, turn the engine over slowly several times, raising the exhaust-valve lifter momentarily and just enough to ease the piston over full compression. Having caused a very rich mixture to be sucked into the combustion chamber, kick the engine over as fast as possible with the exhaust-valve lifter kept fully raised all the time. This should free the piston and enable a start to be effected in the normal manner as described hereafter.

Avoid excessive preliminary sucking in of petrol as this is apt to wet the plug and perhaps break down the oil film completely. In cold weather it is best, where practicable, to keep your Panther in a slightly heated atmosphere.

Where the engine is not stiff due to cold weather conditions it is generally sufficient to set the engine controls as described in the preceding instructions 1-6. Then bring the decompressor (Fig. 3) into operation. Move the lever *upwards* (anti-clockwise) as far as possible, having first raised the exhaust-valve lifter. As soon as the decompressor lever is *right home*, release the exhaust-valve lifter. Now operate the kick-starter smartly. The engine should fire after the second kick (first put engine on compression.) Provided that the decompressor is fully raised, no kick-back is possible. Immediately the engine fires, push the decompressor lever *right down* with the foot as shown in Fig. 3. Also progressively open the air lever until it is wide open and the engine runs smoothly. Move the ignition lever (where fitted) to give a moderately fast tick-over. See also page 16.

Always Use the Stand. Always start up from cold with your Panther model supported on its stand. All 1938 and later Panthers have the excellent P. & M. rolling-type rear or centre stand. Place

Fig. 3. Pushing Decompressor Out of Action with Foot After Starting
(*By courtesy "Motor Cycle," London*)

your foot on one of the cam-type feet and then roll the machine gently back on to its stand.

Starting Up (Engine Warm). Where an engine has already warmed up to its normal working temperature, it should start readily at the first kick. This is assuming you have not flooded the carburettor, have closed the throttle (to idling position, determined by throttle stop), have the air lever fully open, and have moved the ignition lever (where fitted) to the half-advance position to prevent kick-back.

To effect a first-kick start, it is generally sufficient to turn the engine over until the piston is just over full compression (using the exhaust-valve lifter) and then give a decisive, vigorous kick.

It may be mentioned incidentally that it is possible to start up a hot engine *by hand* if the decompressor is first brought into use by raising the lever. The application of the foot is, of course, generally more convenient.

Should Engine Refuse to Start. If your engine is obstinate and refuses to start up from cold after three to four sharp kicks, do not continue. Check that the control setting *is* correct, and remember that a very small throttle opening *must* be used to enable a high-velocity air stream to be induced over the pilot jet.

Verify that petrol *is* actually reaching the float chamber, by observing the effect of depressing the tickler. See that continuous flooding is not taking place, accompanied by petrol dripping from the base of the carburettor. To clear the engine of an over-rich mixture, kick the engine over several times with the air lever wide open and the exhaust-valve lifter raised.

If the petrol supply seems to be in order, unscrew the sparking plug, clean it, verify the gap between the electrodes, and test the plug before replacing it (see page 45). If the plug is in poor condition, fit a new one of the correct type (see page 44).

If the Engine Catches Fire. In the very unlikely event of the carburettor catching fire due to a sticking inlet valve or a backfire (practically impossible if the decompressor is used) immediately close the petrol tap, open the throttle fully and kick the engine over several times with the exhaust-valve lifter raised. Alternatively run the engine fast so as to use up the petrol in the float chamber.

Warming Up Your Panther. As soon as your engine springs into life, set the controls to give a nice tick-over on the pilot jet. Avoid racing the engine immediately after starting up from cold because it takes an appreciable time for the engine oil to warm up and circulate efficiently. Permitting the engine to run very fast when not under load subjects the engine to severe stresses and also generates excessive heat.

Also avoid warming up the engine too slowly and for more than a few minutes. Unless the engine is turning over at a reasonable rate, the oil pump cannot be expected to work fast enough to ensure thorough lubrication at a time when this is *most* essential.

Excessively slow warming up is also apt to result in the incomplete combustion of a cold mixture, with the result that some of the fuel condenses on, and corrodes, the cylinder walls. This detrimental phenomenon is generally referred to as *low-temperature condensation*. Stop warming up when the engine reaches its normal running temperature.

ON THE ROAD

Mount the machine, ease the machine gently off its rear or centre stand, with the gear-change pedal in *neutral* and let the engine run at a moderately fast pace.

To Engage Bottom (First Gear). After warming the engine disengage the clutch by operating the lever on the handlebars (see Fig. 2). Now with the toe of the foot *raise* the foot gear-change pedal *fully* and engage first gear (see Fig. 4). To facilitate

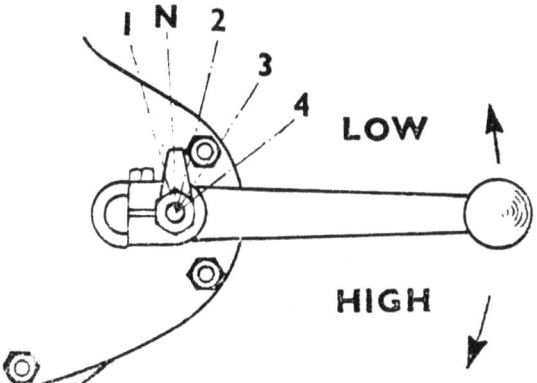

Fig. 4. The Gear-change Sequence as Shown by the Indicator
The pedal itself always returns to the position shown.

proper engagement, it may be necessary to move the Panther slightly backwards or forwards. Remove the toe from the pedal immediately you *feel* that first gear is engaged.

On a New Machine. Some initial difficulty in engaging first gear may be caused by sticking clutch plates, but this trouble quickly disappears with use. If you do experience such difficulty, stop your engine and kick it over sharply several times with the exhaust-valve lifter raised and the clutch fully disengaged.

Moving Off. Having engaged bottom (first) gear, allow the transmission to take up the drive by progressively and gently releasing the clutch lever, when you will move off. As you accelerate and the engine takes the full load, gradually increase the throttle opening with the twist-grip, so as to obtain a progressive increase in the speed of the engine and machine. On 1938-46 and late 1950 and subsequent models with manual control of the ignition, see that the ignition lever is moved as soon as possible to the *full-advance* position.

Changing Up (**First to Second**). When you have accelerated to 12–15 m.p.h.* in bottom gear, change up into second gear. The knack of gear changing is soon mastered, and gear crashing is impossible with the Burman constant-mesh gearbox.

Disengage the clutch and simultaneously throttle down the engine slightly, pause a second, and then *depress* the gear-change pedal to its *full extent* with the toe, until you feel second gear engage (see Fig. 4). Immediately afterwards re-engage the clutch and remove your toe from the gear-change pedal and allow the lever to return to its normal (horizontal) position. Also throttle up the engine slightly, to compensate for the increased load.

Changing Up (**to Third and Top**). Increase the throttle opening progressively until you have accelerated to 20–25 m.p.h.* Then, as before, disengage the clutch, slightly close the throttle, pause a second, and smartly, but without force, *depress* the foot gear-change pedal to its *full extent* until third gear is felt to engage (see Fig. 4). Now re-engage the clutch, remove the toe from the pedal, and throttle up the engine to take up the increased load and maintain a good road speed without any tendency to knock.

To change into top (fourth) gear, accelerate until 30–35 m.p.h.* has been reached, and then repeat the gear changing procedure already described for third gear.

Changing Down (**Top to Third**). Throttle down the engine until your Panther is travelling at a speed normal for third gear. Disengage the clutch, open the throttle slightly, pause a second, and then *raise* the gear-change pedal to its *full extent* with the toe of the foot until you feel third gear engage. Re-engage the clutch immediately afterwards, remove the toe from the pedal, and throttle up the engine slightly so as to compensate for the increase in engine speed relative to that of the rear wheel, determined by the gear ratio.

Changing Down (**to Second and First**). The gear changing procedure is similar to that previously described for changing down from top to third gear. During each gear change, raise the gear-change pedal with the toe of the foot to its full extent. Each complete pedal movement engages the next gear in the gear change sequence as shown by the indicator in Fig. 4.

It is not *essential* when changing down from top or third gear into bottom gear to complete the full gear-changing procedure for each intermediate gear, except when hill climbing. An alternative method is to reduce the speed of the machine to a crawl, disengage the clutch and then raise the gear-change pedal

* These speeds apply to Panther models ridden solo or sidecar.

HANDLING A PANTHER 11

to its full extent twice or three times in quick succession, according to whether third or top gear was previously engaged. While doing this, "blip" the engine slightly. Afterwards re-engage the clutch and throttle up to the desired speed.

Obtaining "Neutral." To obtain "neutral" (which lies between first and second gears) it is necessary to engage first gear, bring the Panther to a halt, disengage the clutch, and then depress the foot gear-change pedal *very* slightly. To check that "neutral" is really engaged, re-engage the clutch very gradually.

Make Full Use of Gearbox. Judicious use of the gearbox saves undue wear and tear and also enables you to "get there" with the minimum discomfort and delay. This applies with special emphasis to sidecar outfits. Here are some hints—

1. Do not be lazy with the gear-change lever, but make full and proper use of the four excellent gear ratios.
2. Change gear decisively and quietly. Noisy changing is bad for the gearbox and offensive to the ears.
3. Do not over-rev the engine in the lower gears.
4. Always change gear *before* your Panther starts to labour, and never permit the engine to knock.
5. Do not force your Panther up a steep hill in top gear.
6. When changing gear, always maintain a steady pressure on the gear-change pedal *until the clutch is felt to engage*.
7. Operate the clutch, throttle, and gear-change pedal with a nicely co-ordinated and simultaneous movement.
8. Always check that the gear-change lever *is* in the neutral position *before* moving your Panther off its rear stand.
9. Keep gearbox friction down to the minimum by regular and correct lubrication (dealt with in Chapter III).

Be Careful with Foot Control. To prevent internal damage, never use the foot gear-change pedal roughly. When changing gear, *gently* depress or raise the pedal fully with the toe according to whether you are changing up or down respectively. Keep the foot away from the pedal except when changing. Remember that the pedal always returns to the same position after each gear change, and that neutral is between first and second gears.

Use Both Brakes Together. To ensure powerful braking with even and minimum wear of the tyres and brake linings, cultivate the habit of using *both* brakes together. Avoid excessive and fierce brake application, as this is highly detrimental to the tyres and transmission, and dangerous on wet roads.

Make full use of engine compression when descending hills, as engine compression acts as a very powerful brake. For controlling speed, never declutch or raise the exhaust-valve lifter. The soundest advice is to *drive on the throttle* and employ the brakes as lightly and seldom as possible.

To Stop. For the benefit of the novice it may be mentioned that to make a normal stop on the road, the appropriate procedure is as follows—
1. Shut the throttle twist-grip right back (clockwise).
2. Disengage the clutch fully.
3. Operate the two brakes together, progressively, applying greater hand and foot pressure as the brakes act.
4. Move the gear-change pedal into *neutral* position (Fig. 4) by raising the pedal fully once or several times according to the gear engaged just before changing down (see page 10).

A little practice will soon enable you to execute the above apparently complicated procedure with lightning speed. Practise stopping and gear changing on a quiet road until you feel competent to negotiate traffic on busy main roads.

To Stop Your Engine. After stopping your Panther with the throttle closed (as far as the throttle stop permits), raise the exhaust-valve lifter for a few seconds and your engine will become "dead." Turn off the petrol tap before leaving your machine. When parking a machine by the roadside, keep it under observation or padlock it.

Hints on Hill Climbing. Always keep the engine revolutions as high as possible by making full use of the gearbox, especially where a sidecar is attached. Change down *in good time* and never allow your engine to labour or knock. Keep the throttle well open and on 1938-46, and 1950-66 Panther models with manual ignition control, retard the ignition lever only in order to ward off a knock. Power output is *reduced* by retarding the ignition.

When descending steep hills, close the throttle and open the air lever fully. By doing this you will make full use of engine compression as a brake and also effectively cool the engine. If you want a pleasant sensation, coast down in neutral, but do not do this on a busy road.

Advice on Sidecar Driving. Almost any make of proprietary sidecar can be attached to Model 100, 120 Panthers, which are ideally suited for passenger carrying. On the level it is seldom necessary to use more than half throttle, irrespective of the weight of the passenger or the prevailing winds.

"Hands off" type steering is possible at all speeds; but see that

Panther-Dowty type forks are inflated (see page 117) so that the dots on the sliding members are just apparent with the sidecar outfit *fully loaded*. If the front forks are under-inflated, the steering is not quite so positive as it should be. Over-inflation, on the other hand, is apt to cause the outfit to steer towards the near side. In connexion with the steering, the front forks can readily be altered to give sidecar steering. For sidecar work, the bottom members must be offset towards the *front* as shown (heavier lines) in Fig. 5.

With a sidecar outfit you have to *drive* the machine rather than ride it as in the case of a solo mount, because you cannot

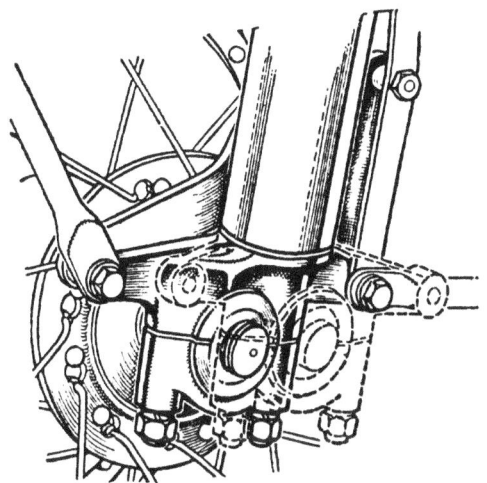

Fig. 5. Alter the Front Forks when Attaching a Sidecar

(*From "Motor Cycle," London*)

The fork spindle housing is offset; by turning the fork bottom members through 180 degrees (after removing front wheel) you can quickly change from solo to sidecar steering and vice versa.

balance it, and the sensation is somewhat different. However, you soon become accustomed to driving a sidecar which is safer on wet roads as it is not so prone to skid. A few hints on sidecar driving are worth noting.

1. On machines with a sidecar attached it is best to keep the steering damper tightened down slightly.

2. Difficulty is sometimes experienced in the management of an empty sidecar when cornering. Ballast substituted for the passenger is of great assistance, and will prevent a tendency for the sidecar to "lift."

3. Be cautious when negotiating left-hand corners. It is

advisable when cornering at speed for the driver to throw his weight slightly towards the left. The safest method of tackling a left-hand corner is to approach the corner at a speed well below that which safety requires, and then open the throttle gradually and cautiously on the bend.

4. When negotiating a right-hand corner, either close the throttle or apply the brakes slightly as the outfit is actually swinging round the bend. It will then pivot on the rear wheel of the motor-cycle itself.

5. Always endeavour to negotiate corners at a reasonable speed, especially when turning to the left, as centrifugal force imposes a considerable lateral strain on the machine. When turning to the right the lateral strain is reversed in direction and has a crushing effect on the sidecar axle via the torque arms.

6. Note that when climbing a steep hill with a sidecar it is not necessary when negotiating a left-hand bend to lean over in that direction, as the natural sidecar side-drag tends to turn the machine to the left.

Sidecar Alignment. If a sidecar outfit has a tendency to steer to the right or left owing to reasons other than road camber or incorrect front-fork inflation, it is possible that the motor-cycle leans outwards excessively, or else the sidecar itself is out of alignment (see page 131).

Use of Steering Damper. On a sidecar outfit, the damper should be kept tightened down moderately tight for all speeds, but on a solo mount it should be used only when travelling over rough road surfaces and when riding at high speeds.

Remember when throttling down to a slow speed always to slacken off the damper, otherwise the machine may develop a tendency for "lurching" and become somewhat difficult to handle.

Always Run on Main Fuel Supply. For obvious reasons it is important to maintain a reserve fuel supply in the petrol tank. Make a habit of always running with the *near-side* petrol tap turned on (see page 5). Keep the off-side petrol tap shut.

Run on a Suitable Plug. To obtain the best all-round performance from your Panther engine it is essential always to use a suitable sparking plug. Suitable plugs for the 598 c.c. and 645 c.c. engines fitted to Panther Models 100 and 120 are the 14 mm, ½ in. reach, K.L.G. F70, F75 or DF75, the Lodge HN or HNP, and the Champion L-7. K.L.G. sparking plugs have been fitted by the makers to all new machines for some years. The sparking plug must always be kept thoroughly clean and its gap correctly adjusted (see page 47).

Go Steady for 500 Miles. If you wish to obtain the highest efficiency for the longest possible time from your Panther, it is absolutely imperative to ride it very carefully during the *first* 500 *miles*, assuming that the machine is brand new or reconditioned as new.

Careful running-in gives the working parts the chance to bed down properly and enables the new surfaces to harden and assume a mirror-like gloss, essential to eliminate friction and enable the oil film to spread evenly.

After 500 miles have been covered, riding cautiously, it is permissible to step up the throttle openings *progressively*. You can indulge in short, but not sustained, bursts of speed, making these gradually more frequent as the engine becomes quite free and the initial stiffness disappears. It is generally unwise to employ full throttle for any appreciable period until about 1,500 miles have been covered. Here are some running-in hints—

1. Do not exceed 30 m.p.h. or race the engine during the first 200 miles. You may run occasionally at 40-45 m.p.h. downhill.

2. Avoid giving more than *half throttle* (up hills or on the level) for the first 500 miles.

3. During the first 500 miles do not omit to add upper-cylinder lubricant to the fuel.

4. Do not allow the engine to run at high r.p.m. when idling or on the road, particularly in the lower gears.

5. On no account permit the engine to labour or knock. Change down into a lower gear *before* it commences to labour.

6. If there is any evidence of a new engine beginning to "pull up" (symptom of a seizure being imminent), *at once* declutch and close the throttle.

7. Do not permit the engine to run for more than a few minutes with the machine at rest or jacked up.

8. Keep the engine, gearbox, and the various motor-cycle parts correctly lubricated (for appropriate instructions, see Chapter III). The use of colloidal graphite during running-in is *not* advised.

9. After the running-in period of 500 miles is completed, clean the engine filter and change the oil (see page 33).

After the First 250 Miles. Check the level of oil in the engine sump and also verify a few important adjustments. Some slight bedding-down generally occurs during the early period of a new Panther's life and at about 250 miles it is advisable to check the adjustment of the following: (*a*) both tappets, (*b*) the gaps between the plug and contact-breaker points, (c) the steering-head bearings, (d) the primary and secondary chains, and (e) the brakes; also check over the various external nuts for tightness.

To Prevent Knocking. To prevent knocking (extremely harmful to any engine), during the running-in period and at all other times you should avoid—
1. Riding too slowly in an unsuitable gear.
2. Changing gear too late.
3. Opening the throttle too quickly.
4. Overheating by allowing the engine to run on a large throttle opening for an excessive period without giving the engine a chance to cool down.
5. Advancing ignition (1938-46, 1950-66) excessively at low r.p.m.
6. Riding on too weak a mixture.
7. Allowing the level of oil in the engine sump to fall too low.
8. Permitting the engine to become dirty internally or externally.

Fuel and Oil Consumption. Petrol consumption varies appreciably according to road conditions and the manner in which a Panther is ridden. Continuous fast riding inevitably steps up the petrol consumption. A badly tuned engine, also, increases consumption.

As regards oil consumption, here again riding methods affect the consumption, as do riding with worn engine bearings, a worn cylinder, scoring of the bore, badly-fitting piston rings, etc.

Starting-up Tip (Engine Cold). On page 6 it is mentioned that you should "first put the engine on compression." The O.H.V. Panther engine is a high-compression type, and should you find that rather excessive physical effort is required to kick it over compression (with the decompressor in use), raise the exhaust-valve lifter when engine compression is felt, and turn the engine very slightly forward before commencing to operate the kick-starter.

Note Regarding Passengers. Note that a pillion or sidecar passenger is *not* covered by the usual third-party or comprehensive insurance, except where specifically stated in the policy. Also note that a pillion passenger astride a solo motor-cycle must hold a current "full" driving licence, if the rider of the machine holds only a "provisional" licence. On a sidecar outfit a "learner" *must* be accompanied by a fully qualified passenger *in the sidecar*.

CHAPTER II

THE AMAL CARBURETTOR

THE carburettor's sole object in life is to supply the engine (through the inlet port) continuously with a correctly proportioned mixture (roughly 13 parts of air to 1 of petrol). Once correctly tuned, it is well able to do its work without assistance, and the maintenance required is very small.

Instruments Fitted. The carburettor fitted to the 1938-45 Panthers is a standard flange-fitted needle-jet Amal instrument, and its official type number is 89/014.

On the 1946-54 models a similar carburettor is specified, but it has a different throttle valve (29/3 instead of 29/4) and the carburettor type number is 289C/1A.

All 1955-66 models have an Amal type 376/30 "Monobloc" flange-fitted needle-jet carburettor (see page 108). Both carburettors are semi-automatic in action; it is necessary to close the air lever only when starting from cold.

THE STANDARD CARBURETTOR (1938-54)

Referring to Fig. 6 showing a sectional view of the Amal semi-automatic carburettor, A is the carburettor body or mixing chamber, the upper part of which has a throttle valve B, with jet-needle C attached by a needle clip. The throttle valve regulates the quantity of mixture supplied to the engine.

Passing through the throttle valve is the air valve D, independently operated and serving the purpose of obstructing the main air passage for starting and mixture regulation. Fixed to the underside of the mixing chamber by the union nut E is the jet block F, and interposed between them is a fibre washer to ensure a petrol-tight joint.

On the upper part of the block is the jet-block barrel H, forming a clean through-way. Integral with the jet block is the pilot jet J, supplied through the passage K. The adjustable pilot air-intake L communicates with a chamber, from which issues the pilot outlet M and the by-pass N. A throttle stop (see Fig. 7) is provided on the mixing chamber, by which the position of the throttle valve for tick-over is regulated independently of the cable adjustment.

The needle jet O is screwed in the underside of the jet block, and carries at its bottom end the main jet *P*. Both these jets are removable when the jet plug *Q*, which bolts the mixing chamber and the float chamber together, is removed. The float chamber,

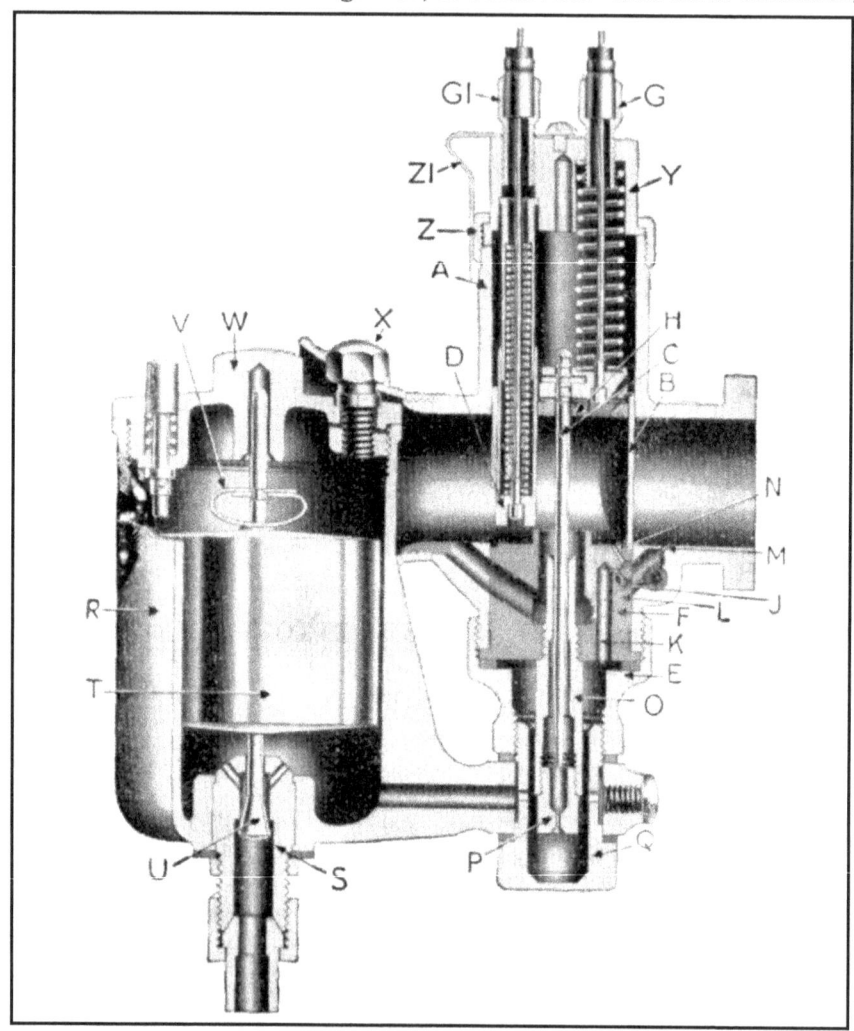

FIG. 6. SECTIONAL VIEW OF AMAL NEEDLE-JET TWO-LEVER SEMI-AUTOMATIC CARBURETTOR
Fitted to all 1938-54 heavyweight Panthers.

which has bottom feed, consists of a cup *R* supplied with petrol through union *S*. It has a float *T* and the needle valve *U* attached by the clip *V*. The float-chamber cover *W* has a lock-screw *X* for security.

The petrol tap having been turned on, petrol will flow past the needle valve U until the quantity of petrol in the chamber R is sufficient to raise the float T, when the needle valve U will prevent a further supply entering the float chamber until some in the chamber has already been used by the engine.

The float chamber having filled to its correct level, the fuel passes along the passages through the diagonal holes in the jet plug Q, when it will be in communication with the main jet P, and the pilot feed-hole K; the level in the needle and pilot jets is, obviously, the same as that maintained in the float chamber.

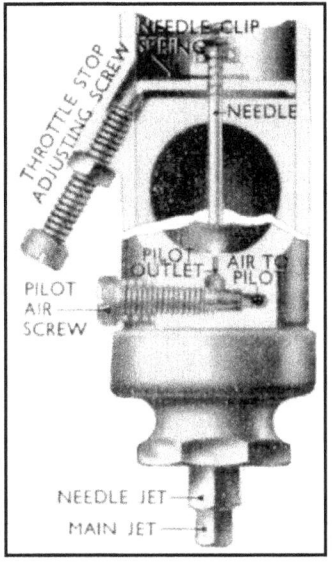

Imagine the throttle valve B very slightly open. As the piston descends, a partial vacuum is created in the carburettor, causing a rush of air through the pilot air-hole L and drawing fuel from the pilot jet J. The mixture of air and fuel is admitted to the engine through the pilot outlet M.

The quantity of mixture capable of being passed by the pilot outlet M is insufficient to run the engine. This mixture also carries excess of fuel. Consequently, before a combustible mixture is admitted, throttle valve B must be slightly raised, admitting a further supply of air from the main air-intake.

FIG. 7. THROTTLE-STOP AND PILOT AIR SCREW

The farther the throttle valve is opened, the less will be the depression on the outlet M, but, in turn, a higher depression will be created on the by-pass N, and the pilot mixture will flow from this passage as well as from the outlet M.

The mixture supplied by the pilot and by-pass system is supplemented at about one-eighth throttle by fuel from the main jet P, the throttle valve cut-away determining the mixture strength from here to one-quarter throttle. Proceeding up the throttle range, mixture control by the needle position occurs from one-quarter to three-quarters throttle, and from this point the main jet is the only regulation.

The air valve D, which is cable-operated on the two-lever carburettor, has the effect of obstructing the main through-way and, in consequence, increasing the depression on the main jet, enriching the mixture. Two cable adjusters, G $G1$, are provided.

The Throttle-stop Screw. The throttle-stop adjusting screw (shown in Fig. 7) is normally adjusted so as to prop the throttle slide open sufficiently to enable the engine to tick-over when the throttle twist-grip is completely closed.

The Pilot Air Screw. This controls the suction imposed on the pilot jet by metering the volume of air which mixes with the fuel. It controls the strength of the mixture for "idling" and also for initial throttle openings.

On Model 100 Panthers with type 89/014 Amal carburettor (1938-45) the air for the pilot jet is admitted externally. In the case of Model 100 Panthers with type 289C/1A Amal carburettor (1946-54) internal admission of air to the pilot jet is provided.

The Main Jet. This regulates the fuel supply at throttle openings exceeding three-quarters full open. At smaller openings of the throttle, the fuel supplied passes through the main jet, but the amount is decreased owing to the needle in the needle jet having a metering effect. The main jet is screwed into the needle jet and can readily be detached after removing the jet plug shown at Q in Fig. 6. Referring to Fig. 7, to remove the main jet, hold the needle jet with one spanner, and with another unscrew the main jet.

Each Amal main jet is numbered and calibrated so that its precise discharge is known. It thus follows that any two main jets having the same number are identical in all respects. The larger the jet, the higher is its number. If a larger size jet is needed, on no account attempt to ream the existing jet, but obtain a new one of larger size. Recommended jet sizes are given on page 22.

The Needle and Needle Jet. The needle is attached to, and moves with, the throttle slide. Being tapered, it permits more or less fuel to pass through the needle jet as the throttle is opened, or closed, respectively. This applies throughout the range of throttle openings, except at nearly full throttle and when "idling." The needle jet is of a specified size, and normally it should not be changed except when going over to alcohol fuels.

As may be seen in Fig. 7, the position of the taper needle relative to the throttle opening can be adjusted according to the mixture required by securing the needle to the throttle with the needle spring-clip in a particular groove, five of which are provided. Position No. 3, for example, means the third groove *from the top*. At throttle openings from one-quarter to three-quarters open, raising the needle enriches the mixture, while lowering the needle weakens it. The needle itself is made in *one size only*.

The Throttle-valve Cut-away. The throttle on the atmospheric side is cut-away, and this affects the depression on the main fuel supply. The cut-away provides a means of tuning between the pilot and needle jet range of throttle opening. The actual amount of cut-away is denoted by a number marked on the throttle slide. Thus 6/4 means a throttle type 6 with a No. 4 cut-away. A throttle with a larger cut-away (say, 6/5) *weakens* the mixture. A smaller cut-away, on the other hand, makes the mixture *richer*.

TUNING STANDARD CARBURETTOR (1938-54)

All 1938 and later Panthers have their carburettors carefully tuned by experts before leaving the P. & M. factory, and as a

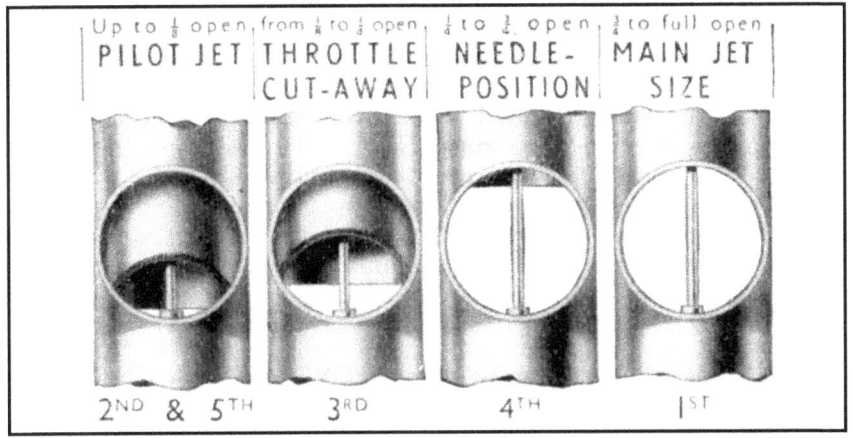

SEQUENCE OF TUNING

FIG. 8. TUNING PROCEDURE

rule it is not wise to meddle with the maker's original setting. Where the original setting has been tampered with, or for other reasons, superior performance may occasionally be obtained by fitting a slightly larger-size main jet, or effecting other adjustments. The pilot jet often needs adjustment for slow running.

Observe Condition of Exhaust. Where the carburettor is correctly tuned, there should be no evidence of black smoke emerging from the exhaust(s). The combustion of fuel is complete and carbon formation almost non-existent. Also where the mixture is right, the exhaust flame is of a *whitish-blue* colour.

If the mixture tends to be weak, the colour of the exhaust flame is *light blue*. If, on the other hand, the mixture is excessively rich, the flame is of a characteristic *yellow* colour, and some *black* smoke is generally present. Note that the above references to exhaust flames imply exhaust flames as observed at an *open* exhaust port.

Tuning Procedure. If the carburettor setting (see accompanying table) on your Panther does not give complete satisfaction for particular requirements, there are four separate ways of rectifying matters as given herewith, and the adjustments should be made in this order—
1. Main jet ($\frac{3}{4}$ to full throttle).
2. Pilot air adjustment (closed to $\frac{1}{8}$ throttle).
3. Throttle valve cut-away on the air-intake side ($\frac{1}{8}$ to $\frac{1}{4}$ throttle).
4. Needle position ($\frac{1}{4}$ to $\frac{3}{4}$ throttle).

The diagram (Fig. 8) clearly indicates the part of the throttle range over which each adjustment is effective.

The carburettor is, throughout the throttle range, entirely automatic, and the air lever should be kept wide open, except for starting and until the engine has warmed up properly. It is assumed that normal petrol is used for tuning, which should be done in the sequence described below. Throttle openings to be used in the five tuning operations are those indicated in Fig. 8. By following these tuning instructions (recommended by Amal, Ltd.) you will be assured of obtaining the most satisfactory performance with maximum economy of fuel. For tuning purposes it is advisable to start up on a quiet road having a slight up gradient, so as to impose a small load on the engine.

1. To Check Size of Main Jet. Accelerate up to full throttle and carefully note the response of the engine to twist-grip action.

AMAL CARBURETTOR SETTINGS FOR
598 C.C. PANTHERS
(1938-54 Solo and Sidecar Models)

Panther Model	Amal Carburettor	Main Jet	Taper Needle	Needle Position	Throttle Valve
100 (1938-45)	89/014	220	T-29-Std.	3	29/4*
100 (1946-54)	289C/1A	220	T-29-Std.	3	29/3

* A 29/4 throttle valve was fitted as standard on all 1938-45 Panthers, but a 29/3 valve was fitted by Messrs. Amal, Ltd., to 1946 and later models at the request of Messrs. Phelon & Moore, Ltd. For all renewals, use a 29/3 valve. For 1955-66 settings, see page 109.

Should power output appear better with the air lever very slightly closed or with the throttle not completely open, this indicates that the main jet is too small, and the next larger size should be tried. Similarly, if there is a tendency for the engine to run "heavily" on full throttle, this denotes that the main jet is too large and the next smaller size should be experimented with.*

If tuning for speed, be careful to choose a main jet of size sufficient to maintain the engine in a cool condition. Make a run at high speed, pull up, and stop the engine immediately. Remove the sparking plug and closely inspect it. If the business end of the plug is sooty, the mixture is too rich. Should the body be dry or grey in colour, the mixture is on the weak side, and a larger size jet is required.

With a properly proportioned mixture, the plug body should have a bright black appearance. Also, when running, observe the sound of the exhaust; it should be crisp and have no trace of "wooliness." Black smoke at the exhaust shows that the mixture is much too rich.

2. To Adjust the Pilot Jet. Allow the engine to idle at an excessive speed, with the twist-grip closed and the air lever wide open. The ignition lever (1938-46, 1951-4 models) should be set to obtain the best slow-running.

Loosen the nut on the throttle-stop screw, and unscrew the latter until the engine slows up and begins to stall. Then screw the pilot-air screw in or out as required to enable the engine to run regularly and faster. To weaken the mixture screw the pilot-air screw *outwards*.

Next, gently lower the throttle-stop screw until the engine again begins to falter. Now lock the throttle-stop screw with the lock-nut and commence to readjust the pilot-air screw to obtain the optimum slow-running. Should this second adjustment cause the engine to tick-over at an excessive speed, repeat the adjustment a third time. When perfect slow-running has been obtained, tighten the lock-nut on the throttle-stop screw without disturbing the position of the screw. See also page 109.

3. The Throttle Cut-away. Should appreciable spitting-back at the carburettor occur on accelerating from rest with the engine idling, stop the machine and slightly enrich the mixture by screwing the pilot-air screw in approximately *half a turn*. If this does not effect the desired result, screw it back to its former position and fit a throttle slide having a smaller cut-away.

If there is no spitting-back but the engine jerks under load, this shows an over-rich mixture, and the remedy is to fit a throttle slide with larger cut-away, or else to lower the throttle needle.

* Different size jets are obtainable from Amal spares stockists, or from Amal, Ltd., Holdford Road, Witton, Birmingham, 6.

4. Jet-needle Position. The tapered needle influences a wide range of throttle openings and affects acceleration. Check performance with the needle in as low a position as possible, i.e. with the clip in the groove nearest the end of the needle. If acceleration of your Panther declines, and improves by partially closing the air lever, raise the position of the needle by two grooves. If a marked improvement is thereby obtained, try the effect of lowering the needle, by one groove, and leave it in the position where the best performance is obtained.

It should be noted that if the mixture is still excessively rich with the needle clip in groove No. 1 (nearest the end), wear of the needle jet has probably occurred and renewal of the jet is called for. The needle itself is of stainless steel and wear does not take place, even after a big mileage.

5. Verify the Idling Adjustment. Also make any final small adjustment which is required to obtain perfectly smooth tickover, neither too fast nor too slow (see page 8).

Pilot Jet Obstructed. If the pilot-jet adjustment does not obtain the desired results and the engine will not idle nicely with the throttle almost closed, the air lever pulled fully open, and the ignition lever (where fitted) about two-thirds advanced, the pilot jet may be obstructed. The jet passage, actually a duct drilled in the jet block, is very small and can easily become choked.

To gain access to the pilot jet, remove the jet plug Q and the float chamber R (see Fig. 6), and then detach the jet block by pushing it out of the mixing chamber. The pilot jet can then be cleared (see page 26).

Poor Slow-running. If it is found impossible to obtain good slow-running by making the pilot-air adjustment as described in the second operation on page 23, it is probable that some defect other than carburation is responsible for preventing the engine running slowly at low revolutions. Air leaks are a possible cause which should be looked for (see page 25). Badly-seating valves will also weaken the mixture. Defects in the ignition system may also be responsible for poor tick-over. The sparking plug may be oily, or the points set too close (see page 46). Possibly the spark is excessively advanced or the contact-breaker needs attention (see page 49). Examine the slip-ring for oil and see that the pickup brush is bedding down and in good condition. Also examine the h.t. cable for signs of shorting.

If Consumption of Fuel is High. If, in spite of careful checking up on the tuning of the carburettor, high fuel consumption

THE AMAL CARBURETTOR

continues, it is likely that one or more of the under-mentioned causes is responsible for wastage of precious fuel. Late ignition timing will eat into your petrol supplies quickly. The same applies to poor engine-compression due to badly fitting piston rings or valves. Also take into consideration the question of flooding due to a faulty float, air leakage at the joint between the carburettor and engine, weak valve springs, worn guides. Wastage can be caused by slack petrol-pipe union nuts.

MAINTENANCE OF YOUR CARBURETTOR

To ensure correct carburation occasionally remove the carburettor from the engine, strip it down completely, and thoroughly clean it. It is a good plan to do this about every 3-4 months.

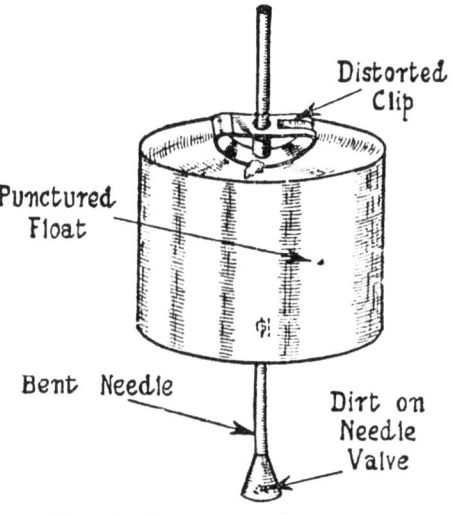

Fig. 9. Possible Causes of Persistent "Flooding"

Dismantling. First detach the petrol feed pipe. Unscrew the jet plug Q (see Fig. 6) and remove the float chamber complete. With box or set spanner, slacken the mixing chamber union nut E. The complete mixing chamber may now be removed from the engine.

To remove chamber, undo the two nuts holding the carburettor flange. Unscrew mixing chamber lock ring Z (held by clip $Z1$), and pull out the throttle valve, needle, and air valve. Remove the main jet P and needle jet O. The mixing-chamber union nut E may then be removed and the jet block completely pushed out. If this is obstinate, tap gently, using a wooden stump inside the mixing chamber. Unscrew the float-chamber cover W, after slackening the lock-screw X. Withdraw the float by pinching the clip V inwards, and pull gently upwards.

Cleaning the Instrument. Wash all components thoroughly clean with petrol. Pay special attention to the float chamber, and see that any impurities collected inside are removed completely.

Inspect Parts Occasionally. If the carburettor has been in continuous service for a considerable period, it is advisable to inspect the following components carefully—

1. FLOAT CHAMBER. Scrutinize the float-chamber components

closely. Hand polish the valve part of the float needle by rotating the needle in its seat while pulling it vertically upwards. If a distinct shoulder is visible on the needle where it seats, renew the needle. Examine the needle for signs of bending.

2. THROTTLE VALVE. Test in the mixing chamber, and if excessive play is present it is advisable to renew the valve without delay.

3. THE JET-NEEDLE CLIP. This part must securely grip the needle. Free rotation must *not* take place, otherwise the needle groove will become worn and necessitate a new part being fitted. Be sure to refit the clip in the correct groove.

4. JET BLOCK. If trouble has been experienced with erratic "idling," ascertain by blowing or with a fine bristle that the pilot jet J (see Fig. 6) is clear, and that the pilot outlet M in the mixing chamber is unobstructed.

Assembling the Carburettor. Referring to Fig. 6, refit the jet block F with a washer on the underside, and screw on lightly the mixing-chamber union nut E. Screw in needle jet O and main jet P. Open air lever $\frac{7}{8}$ in., and throttle grip half-way; grasp the air slide between the thumb and the finger; *make sure that the jet needle enters the central hole in the barrel H*. Slightly turn the throttle valve until it enters the barrel guide, when, on pushing down the valves, the air valve should enter its guide. If not, slightly move the mixing-chamber cap Y, when the air valve will slide into place. Screw on the mixing chamber lock-ring Z. No force is necessary.

Attach the carburettor to the cylinder, pushing it right home, and examine the washer of the flange joint. Insert the jet plug Q and thoroughly tighten the union nut E by means of a fixed spanner. Refit float and needle, holding the needle head against its seating by means of a pencil, until the float and the clip V are slipped into position. Make sure that the clip enters the groove provided. Screw on the cover tightly and lock in position by means of the lock-screw X. The float-chamber jet plug Q has one washer above and one beneath the lug. Screw the jet plug into union nut E and lock it securely. Clean the petrol pipe and filter, if fitted, and replace. It will be necessary to re-check the pilot setting if this has been disturbed (see page 24).

Wear of Needle Jet. See notes on page 24.

Air Filters. The maintenance of air filters (two types) fitted to Model 100, 120 Panthers is dealt with on pages 112-13.

CHAPTER III
CORRECT LUBRICATION

YOUR Panther will maintain its tune and "kick" and give you trouble-free running almost indefinitely, provided that you are not neglectful in regard to its maintenance, and especially lubrication.

ENGINE LUBRICATION

The underlying principle of all engine lubrication systems is to avoid friction (and the consequent heat generation) between all moving surfaces by maintaining between them an oil film which just keeps the surfaces apart. The circulating oil also helps to convey heat away from the combustion chamber and piston.

To obtain correct (or rather approximately correct) lubrication, you must always—

(a) Use suitable engine oil of the correct grade.
(b) Maintain sufficient oil in constant circulation.
(c) Keep the oil clean and undiluted.

Panther Semi-wet Sump Lubrication. The same type of engine lubrication system is provided on all Model 100 and 120 Panthers. Known as a "semi-wet sump" system, it combines the advantages of both wet- and dry-sump systems.

The lubrication system is designed so that the quantity of engine oil inside the crankcase never exceeds the amount which just contacts the flywheel rims. Thus the oil drag on the two flywheels when starting up from cold is scarcely greater than with a full dry-sump system.

The scavenging capacity of the oil pump is not (as on full dry-sump systems) greater than the delivery capacity, and therefore some oil is always left in the crankcase when the engine stops. Consequently some splash lubrication occurs when starting up from cold and when circulation is sluggish prior to the engine attaining its normal working temperature.

The oil-circulation diagram (Fig. 10) shows how the oil circulates in the Panther engine which has a sump (capacity ½ gal.) cast integral with the crankcase but not in communication with it. Oil is drawn upwards from the sump through a suction pipe by a double-ended reciprocating pump, incorporated in the larger (idler) gear inside the timing case. On its way upwards to the pump the oil percolates through a large gauze filter (see Figs. 10 and 14). The pump then forces the oil at a pressure of about

10 lb. per sq. in. through ducts in the crankcase to the double-row roller big-end bearing, also through a duct in the cylinder barrel to a point at the rear of the piston. Some of the oil is fed to the timing gears.

An external pipe leads from the pump (top of the timing case actually) to the rocker-box and feeds the overhead rocker

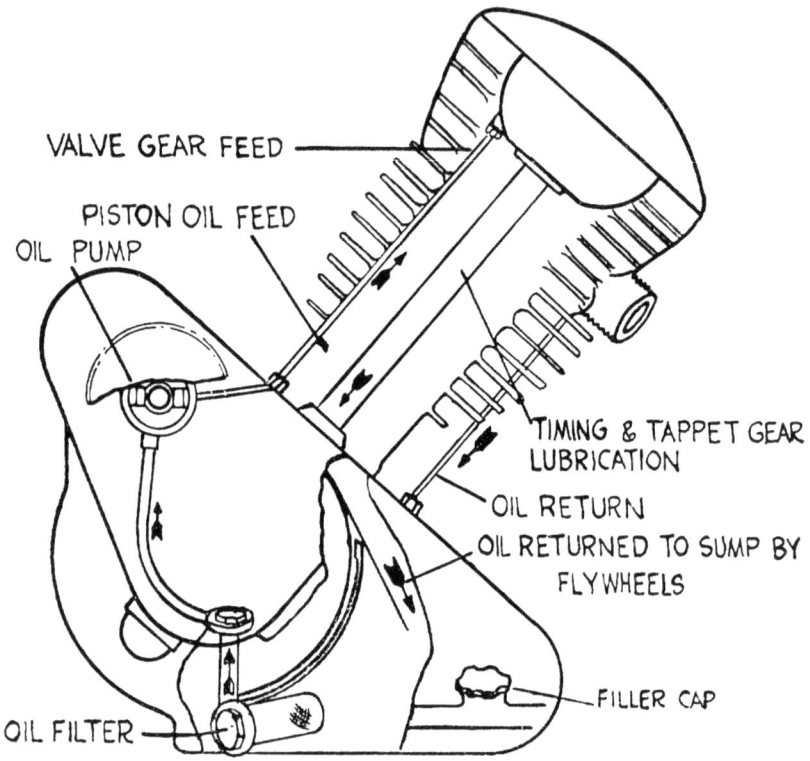

FIG. 10. PANTHER OIL-CIRCULATION DIAGRAM
Applies to all Model 100 and 120 engines.

bearings. After lubricating the bearings, oil is returned by an external pipe to the crankcase. Some of it, however, returns by gravity down the push-rod cover tube and helps to lubricate the tappets and timing gear.

All surplus oil in the engine is returned eventually to the base of the crankcase, and when the oil accumulates sufficiently therein to contact the rims of the flywheels it is carried round and projected through a slit into the oil sump for further circulation. The crankcase is well ventilated and considerable external finning is provided to keep the oil reasonably cool.

CORRECT LUBRICATION

To enable you to maintain sufficient oil in circulation, a combined filler cap and dip-stick is incorporated at the forward end of the crankcase on the off side. Also on the off side, on top of the timing case, is a metal cap. Removal of this cap gives access to an adjustable screw (see Fig. 11) for the oil-pressure relief valve. If the oil pressure rises to about 20 lb. per sq. in.,

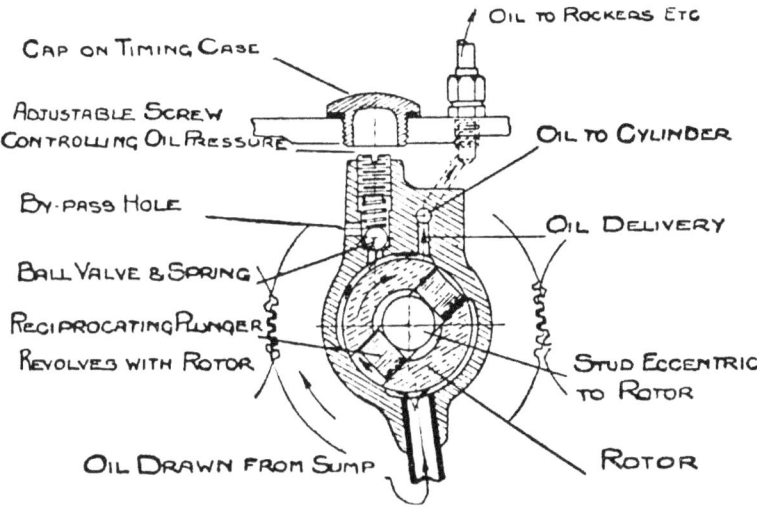

FIG. 11. SECTIONAL VIEW OF OIL PUMP
(ALL 1938-66 ENGINES)

surplus oil is automatically by-passed through a hole to the timing gears.

In the event of the engine exhibiting symptoms of excessive lubrication (becoming dirty and tending to "smoke") an adjustment of the relief valve (see page 31) can readily be made. No other adjustment is included in the Panther lubrication system.

The Oil Pump. This is a double-ended reciprocating plunger-type oil pump with no valves other than an oil-pressure relief valve. The general arrangement of the pump may be understood by reference to Figs. 11 and 12, which show the pump assembled and dismantled respectively.

Referring to Fig. 12, the annular-shaped pump body A is flange-fitted to the timing-case wall. The pump rotor which forms the integral boss of the intermediate timing gear B fits closely inside the bore of the pump body which serves as a bearing. The rotor is also drilled axially, and at right angles to the large centre hole are two smaller holes drilled to form bearings for the double-ended pump plunger D.

Engaging the centre recessed portion of the pump plunger *D* is a stud fixed to the timing case eccentrically to the rotor of the intermediate gear *B*. Thus, rotation of the rotor imparts a reciprocating motion to the pump plunger, which thus functions as a double-acting pump.

As the pump plunger moves outwards in the two bearing holes of the rotor, a vacuum is created in one bearing hole because both

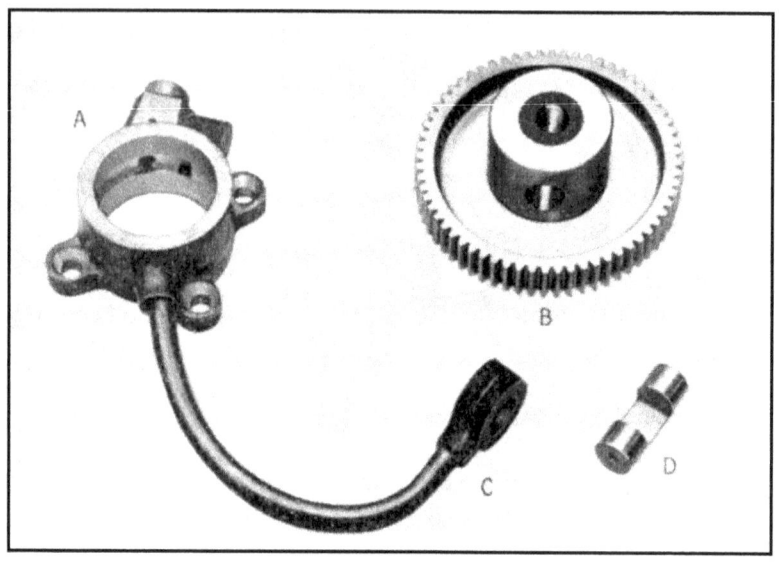

Fig. 12. Oil-pump Components (1938 onwards)
A. Pump body (oil-pressure relief valve housing at top).
B. Intermediate timing gear with integral rotor.
C. Suction pipe (leading from oil filter).
D. Oil-pump plunger (engaging stud eccentric to rotor).

the plunger and the rotor fit closely in their housings. This vacuum occurs just as the reciprocating plunger passes over a groove (communicating with the suction pipe *C*) cut in the lower part of the pump body bore. Oil is consequently drawn up from the sump reservoir via the filter and suction pipe and completely fills both the groove and the space vacated by the oil-pump plunger. As the pump rotor further rotates, the end of the groove is passed and the oil accumulated between the bore of the pump body and the plunger is trapped.

On reaching the limit of its outward movement, the pump plunger begins to reverse its movement, and in so doing forces the trapped oil through a small opening drilled at the top of the bore of the pump body. This opening is the right-hand one of the two which can be observed in Fig. 12. The other opening communicates with the oil-pressure relief valve. The oil is forced through the right-hand opening through the main oil-way to the big-end bearing and the rear of the cylinder wall.

Some of the oil is by-passed to the timing gears and overhead rockers, as already mentioned (see page 28). In turn, each end of the pump plunger executes first a suction and then a delivery stroke. The rotor rotates at 0·375 times the engine speed.

Regulation of Oil Pressure. No adjustment is necessary or provided (1938 onwards) to vary the volume of oil fed to the engine by the oil pump. But, as mentioned on page 29, it is possible to regulate the oil pressure by means of an adjustable screw situated above the oil-pressure relief valve (see Fig. 11). The maker's setting of the screw should *not* normally be interfered with and allows the oil to raise the spring-loaded ball and some oil to by-pass to the timing gears when a pressure of about 20 lb. per sq. in. is attained. The average oil pressure on the delivery side of the oil pump is around 10 lb. per sq. in.

Should an engine show symptoms of insufficient or excessive oil pressure with high oil consumption, even after the first 1,000 miles, it is desirable to adjust the pressure. Incidentally, wear of the piston, cylinder, rings, bearings, etc., decreases the pressure. Adjust with the engine *warm* at a fast tick-over.

To make an oil-pressure adjustment, apply a screwdriver to the slotted adjustable screw after first removing the metal cap (with engine stopped) from the top of the timing case. Turn the screw slightly clockwise or anti-clockwise to increase or decrease the oil pressure respectively. Verify before reducing the oil pressure that the crankcase air-release valve (see page 34) is not faulty. Lubrication is correct when oil slowly trickles from the oil feed pipe to the rocker-box with the upper union disconnected.

To Check Oil Circulation. The engine lubrication system on 1938 and later engines is almost fool-proof, and it is rarely necessary to check the oil circulation, if the oil sump is kept properly replenished.

In the unlikely event of the engine running "dry" because of some obstruction in the circulation system, you can check that the oil *is* being circulated by the pump by removing the plug screwed into the crankcase at the end of the cylinder-wall oil feed to the rear of the piston. If the oil is circulating, it will be observed to issue, when the engine is running, from the plug hole. Alternatively slacken or disconnect one end of the external oil-feed pipe to the rocker-box. The pipe concerned is the rear one.

Suitable Engine Oils. Always replenish from branded cabinets or sealed containers, and never use an inferior or unsuitable oil which may result in a worn or damaged cylinder, piston, bearings, etc.

Phelon & Moore, Ltd., advise the exclusive use of one of the following five engine oils—

1. Castrol XXL (summer) or XL (winter).
2. Shell X-100 40 (summer) or 30 (winter).
3. Mobiloil AF (summer) or A (winter).
4. Essolube 40 (summer) or 30 (winter).
5. B.P. Energol SAE 40 (summer) or Energol SAE 30 (winter). See also page 43.

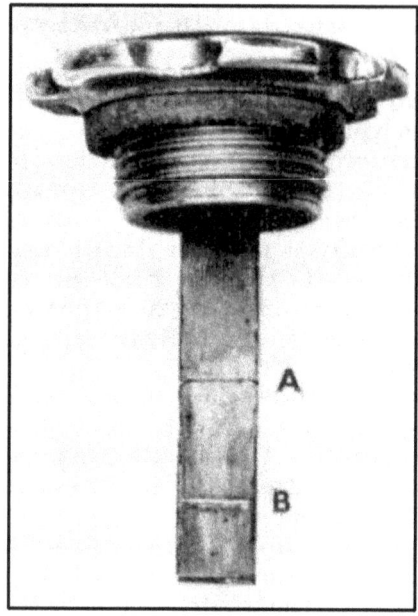

FIG. 13. COMBINED FILLER CAP AND DIP-STICK (1938-66)

Check Oil Level in Sump Every 250 Miles. As mentioned on page 43, the oil sump of a new machine should be replenished with about four pints of one of the engine oils just referred to. Thereafter check the level of oil in the sump about every 250 miles and top-up when necessary. To ensure that the oil is kept as pure and cool as possible never permit the oil level to fall too low.

To check the oil level, unscrew the combined filler cap and dip-stick, situated low down towards the front on the off side of the crankcase, and observe the position of the top of the oil film adhering to the dip-stick. As may be seen in Fig. 13, the dip-stick blade has two notches. Do not fill the oil sump to the brim, as this tends to cause over lubrication through oil rising above the sump baffle.

To obtain correct lubrication, do not allow the oil to rise above the top notch *A* on the dip-stick or to fall below the bottom of the dip-stick. For the best results, keep the oil level between the notch *B* and notch *A* on the dip-stick, preferably as near to *B* as possible. When replenishing the sump be patient and allow the oil to find its *true level* before taking a reading with the dip-stick. It is advisable to top-up the sump after stopping the engine for some time, so as to allow about a pint of oil collected in the timing case to drain back into the sump.

Clean Filter and Change the Oil Every 2,000 Miles. Regular cleaning of the filter and changing of the oil are essential to keep the oil free from dilution and contamination (by carbon and metal particles). This applies particularly during the earlier stages of an engine's life.

On the Panther engine the drain plug and gauze filter are

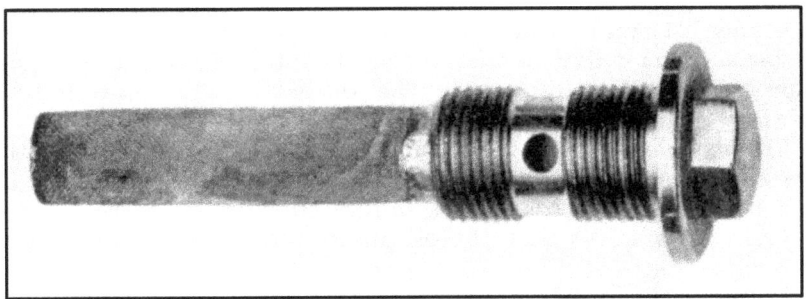

Fig. 14. COMBINED DRAIN PLUG AND GAUZE FILTER (1938-66)
The filter washer is not shown.

combined (see Fig. 14) and, as may be observed from Fig. 10, are situated horizontally at the bottom rear corner of the timing-case side of the oil sump. Always drain the sump after a run when the oil is *warm* and therefore flows freely.

On a new machine remove the combined drain plug and filter after the first 500 miles. Subsequently remove it once every 2,000 miles.* When unscrewing the drain plug be careful not to lose or damage the filter washer, and handle the filter with care as the gauze mesh is readily dented or otherwise damaged. Allow all oil in the sump to drain into a suitable receptacle placed beneath the drain-plug hole.

Wash the gauze filter thoroughly in clean petrol, but do not wipe it with a fluffy rag, or you may block up some of the small holes. It is advisable (but not essential) to flush out the crankcase with a proprietary flushing oil prior to replenishing the sump with 3-4 pints (page 43) of new oil. Use one of the oils recommended on page 32, and replenish to the level of the *top notch* on the dipstick (*A*, Fig. 13). Before commencing to replenish, always verify that the filter washer (between crankcase and drain-plug

---

* The oil should be changed and the filter cleaned when decarbonizing, as it is then likely to be dirty.

flange) is replaced and that the drain plug is tightened down securely.

Lubrication of Overhead Valves, etc. On all engines the external oil-feed pipe from the crankcase to the rocker-box automatically lubricates the overhead valves, etc. No adjustment is included; forget all about the lubrication of overhead rockers, valve guides, push-rods, tappets, etc.

Excessive Lubrication Caused by Faulty Air-release Valve. If excessive engine lubrication occurs, before altering the oil pressure (see page 31) make quite sure that the air-release valve is not at fault. The valve (a metal disc) is integral with the engine-sprocket securing nut inside the oil-bath chain case for the primary chain.

The air-release valve is responsible for releasing and preventing the building-up of air pressure inside the crankcase during the downward piston strokes. Its failure to function correctly may erroneously suggest that the oil pump is feeding excessive oil to the engine.

If the engine tends to "smoke" and some oil leakage occurs, it is possible that the air-release valve disc is sticking, or that dirt is preventing its seating properly. To remedy this, remove the engine-sprocket securing nut and clean it thoroughly in petrol. Eliminate all gumminess, dirt, etc. Shake the nut vigorously; the disc should be quite free to rattle. If it is necessary to remove the disc, you can do this readily after tapping out its split cotter-pin.

Lubrication of B.T.H. " K " Type Magneto (1938 Models). On 1938 models the ball bearings of the B.T.H. magneto armature are packed with grease by the magneto manufacturers during initial assembly, and this is sufficient for about 15,000 miles running.

About every 15,000 miles return the magneto to the British Thomson-Houston Co., Ltd., of Rugby, or to one of their service stations in order to have the instrument overhauled and the bearings regreased.

When occasion is had to remove the contact-breaker for thorough cleaning (see page 51), smear the rocker-arm bearing bush lightly with some thin machine oil. Wipe off all surplus oil liable to get on to the contacts.

The Miller DM3G Dynamo (1938 Models). On 1938 Panthers with B.T.H. "K" type magnetos the bearings of the Miller dynamo are packed with grease during assembly by the dynamo makers, and this is sufficient for 10,000–15,000 miles running.

At regular periods of about 15,000 miles the dynamo should be stripped down, overhauled, and the armature bearings repacked with grease. Preferably this work should be undertaken by H. Miller & Co., Ltd., of Aston Brook Street, Birmingham, 6, or by one of their agents.

An oiler is provided at the driving end of the dynamo; insert a few drops of good quality oil about every 500 miles. The commutator-end bearing is packed with H.M.P. grease by the makers.

Lubrication of Miller " Dyno-mag " (1939-40 Models). The main bearings of the "Dyno-mag" are packed with "high-speed" grease by the makers, and no further attention is normally necessary until a large mileage has been covered (say, 15,000 miles), when the instrument should be returned for a general overhaul to the makers or one of their agents. It is advisable to apply a spot of oil to the cam track occasionally.

The Lucas Type N1 Magneto (1945-51). The ball bearings of the magneto are packed with grease before leaving the makers, and do not require any attention until a general magneto overhaul becomes necessary after a very big mileage.

When regreasing and general overhaul are necessary (at, say, 15,000 miles), remove the magneto from the engine and send or take it to Joseph Lucas, Ltd., of Birmingham, 19, or to a Lucas service depot. Lucas depots in the London area are situated at Dordrecht Road, Acton Vale and at 757-79 High Road, Leyton. No grease nipples or oil holes are provided on the Lucas N1 magneto, but periodical oiling of the contact-breaker is essential.

To Lubricate Contact-breaker of Lucas Type N1 Magneto. The face-cam type contact-breaker is best removed from the magneto as both its cam and tappet require to be lubricated about every 3,000 miles. The following is the procedure recommended—

First remove the spring blade and take off the contact-breaker cover. Then, referring to Fig. 15, remove the screw E and the spring washer retaining the spring arm A to the body of the contact-breaker, and detach the curved backing spring D and the spring arm A. Next unscrew the screw B carrying the lubrication wick, and remove the fibre insulating bush. Straighten the tab on the locking plate situated behind the head of the contact-breaker securing screw H, and with the magneto spanner remove the screw. Then lever off the contact-breaker body from the armature shaft extension.

After removing the contact-breaker, saturate the wick, mounted in the core of the carrying screw B, with a few drops of *thin machine-oil.* Push the tappet from the contact-breaker body and with a soft cloth, wipe the tappet clean. Smear a little thin oil on the tappet and then replace it, or renew if worn.

When reassembling the contact-breaker, proceed in the reverse order of dismantling. See that the curved backing spring *D* is replaced so that the curved part is on the *outside* as shown in Fig. 15.

Lucas Automatic Timing Control (1947-50). The centrifugal type automatic-timing control mechanism is incorporated in the

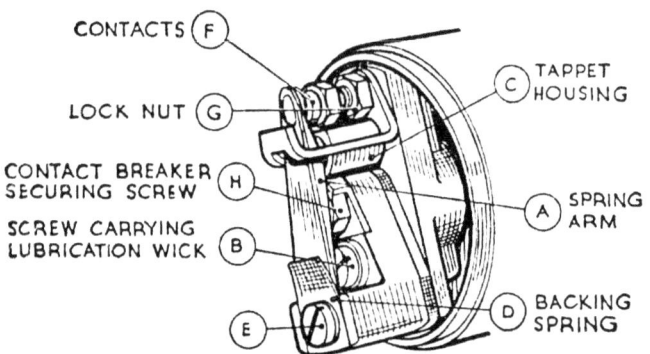

Fig. 15. Face-cam Contact-breaker on Lucas Type N1 Magneto or "Magdyno" (1945 onwards)

"Magdyno" fitted on all late 1951 and subsequent models.

driving gear of the Lucas magneto and is kept adequately lubricated by the oil which lubricates the timing gears.

Lubrication of Lucas E3H and E3L Dynamo (1945-53). On 1945-9 Panthers the ball bearing at the driving end of the E3H dynamo is packed with grease and this should be adequate until a general overhaul (at about every 15,000 miles) is needed. A lubricator, however, is fitted on the commutator end bracket (see Fig. 28) and a few drops of good quality thin machine oil should be inserted about every 1,500 miles.

On 1950-1 Panthers, ball bearings are fitted at *both* ends of the E3L armature, and since these bearings are packed with grease during initial assembly, no further lubrication is necessary, except at general overhauls, undertaken preferably by the makers or at a Lucas service depot.

To Lubricate "Magdyno" (1951 Onwards). Lubricate the contact-breaker of the magneto portion of the "Magdyno" (fitted to late 1951 and subsequent Panthers) about every 3,000 miles

CORRECT LUBRICATION 37

in accordance with the instructions already given (page 35) for the contact-breaker of the Lucas type N1 magneto fitted to 1945-50 and some 1951 Panthers.

As regards the dynamo portion of the Lucas "Magdyno," see the instructions just given for the Lucas separate E3L dynamo fitted to 1950 and some 1951 Panthers.

Grease Dynamo Chain Every 1,000 Miles. Where a separate dynamo (Miller or Lucas) is fitted, the dynamo chain runs in a chain case just behind the rear of the timing case, and is not automatically lubricated. Every 1,000 miles smear the chain with some grease. Grease used for lubricating the various cycle parts (see page 39) is suitable.

THE CYCLE PARTS

While engine lubrication is of primary importance, you must never neglect correct lubrication of the cycle parts.

Burman Gearbox Lubrication. Never replenish the Burman gearbox (type BAP) with thick grease, as this causes difficult gear changing which may damage the gears and dog-type clutches.

The gearbox on all new Panthers is filled by the makers with sufficient lubricant for at least 1,000 miles running. In some instances slight over-filling occurs, and there may be a tendency for some leakage during the first few miles. If this initial leakage does not persist, disregard it.

On 1938-49 3-speed models the filler orifice is revealed on removing a small metal cover on top of the gearbox. About every 1,500-2,000 miles remove the metal cover and insert 2-3 oz. of one of the proprietary *light* greases mentioned on page 39 for cycle parts. Rotating the kick-starter will assist replenishment. Do not insert excessive grease, otherwise some will be forced out of the bearings. Normally keep the gearbox about *one-third* full. Shell Spirax C is also suitable.

On 1950-66 4-speed models unscrew the slotted filler-cap on the off side of the gearbox (see Fig. 55) about every 1,500-2,000 miles and insert 2-3 oz. of *summer grade* engine oil (see page 32). Rotate the kick-starter several times to assist replenishment of the gearbox, which should be replenished so that the level of engine oil is just below the mainshaft (visible when the filler-cap is removed).

When replenishing a 3-speed gearbox with grease, do not forget to grease the enclosed kick-starter and foot gear-change mechanism, where grease nipples are provided. This, of course, does not apply to 1950-66 4-speed models where the parts are automatically lubricated by oil splash.

Change Gearbox Lubricant When Decarbonizing. When undertaking a top overhaul at 3,000-5,000 mile intervals, change the gearbox lubricant. Drain the lubricant off completely, flush out the gearbox with a suitable flushing oil, and afterwards replenish with about 1 lb. 14 oz. of grease (3-speed) or 1¼ pt. of engine oil (4-speed) to just below the mainshaft.

No drain plug is provided, and it is necessary to slacken the

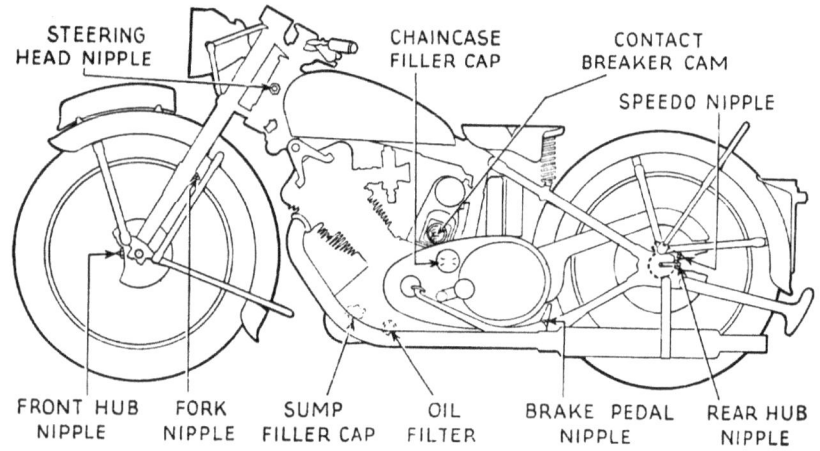

Fig. 16. Location of Main Lubrication Points
(1947 onwards)

On "springers" do not forget the pivot (not shown) for the swinging arm. The fork nipples shown are omitted on 1954-66 models, but on 1938-46 machines nipples are provided for fork-spindle lubrication.

nuts on the gearbox end-cover securing studs on pre-1954 models. Later Burman gearboxes have a drain plug (low down at the rear).

Primary Chain Lubrication. On all 1938 and later models, the primary chain runs totally enclosed in a polished aluminium oil-bath chain case but it receives no lubrication automatically. Only when there is an excessive pressure within the crankcase does oil get blown past the crankcase oil relief-valve disc.

Inspect the level of lubricant in the oil-bath chain case about every 500 miles and verify that the level is sufficient to enable a film of oil to be lifted by the bottom run of the chain. Avoid a high level. If the level is insufficient, top-up the chain case through the inspection-cover hole with *winter grade* engine oil.

Secondary Chain Lubrication. Automatic lubrication of the secondary chain is by an overflow from the oil-bath primary chain case. The overflow operates only when the engine is

CORRECT LUBRICATION

running and is controlled on pre-1957 models by a needle valve in the primary chain case, just behind the clutch dome.

To obtain the best needle-valve setting, note the condition of the chain during a run. Should the chain appear to be running at all dry, increase the overflow by turning the adjuster-needle head *anti-clockwise*. Check the oil supply to the chain about every 500 miles. If dry, smear with some graphite grease.

Occasionally (say, about every 3,000 miles) it is a good plan to remove the secondary chain and immerse it in a bath of paraffin.

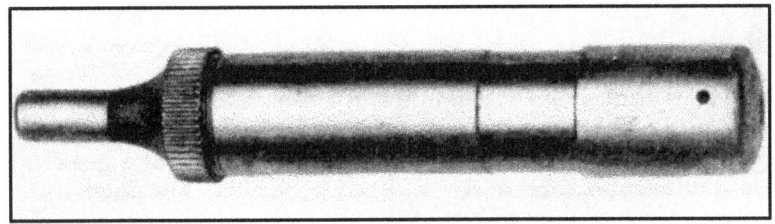

Fig. 17. Tecalemit Grease Gun Supplied in Tool Kit

Allow the chain to soak well to ensure all dirt being removed, and hang the chain up to dry. Then immerse it for at least five minutes in a suitable receptacle containing tallow which has been heated over hot water until molten. Allow all surplus molten tallow to drain off the chain. Finally, fit the chain to the sprockets and see that the spring link is fitted with the *open end* facing away from the direction of chain movement.

Suitable Greases for Motor-cycle Parts. Five suitable greases for lubricating the various motor-cycle parts are—

1. Castrolease CL (Medium for 3-speed gearbox).
2. B.P. Energrease AO.
3. Esso Grease.
4. Mobilgrease No. 2.
5. Shell Retinax A or CD.

Any of the above greases will give excellent results. The grease chosen should be injected when and where required with a suitable grease gun.

Using Grease Gun. The Tecalemit grease gun supplied in the tool kit of all new Panthers is shown in Fig. 17. It should be charged and applied regularly to all grease nipples on the machine (except the wheel hubs) as indicated in the appropriate paragraphs of this chapter.

When preparing the grease gun for use, charge the gun so that the grease is on the top side of the piston. Special grease canisters provided with loose collars having holes are obtainable. To charge the grease gun from one of these canisters, place the barrel of the gun over the hole in the central floating-plate and press down firmly. Turn the grease gun and simultaneously remove it from the floating plate. This procedure should charge the gun such that the grease is flush with the end of its barrel.

Oil Wheel Hubs Every 1,000 Miles. Although grease nipples have been fitted to very many pre-1956 front and rear wheel hubs (suitable oiling caps not being available), grease should *not* be used for lubricating the non-adjustable journal-type ball bearings. About every 1,000 miles inject a small quantity of engine oil (see page 32) through the nipples or caps. Be careful not to inject excessive oil, otherwise some may get on to the brake shoes and impair brake efficiency. Full-width hubs: see page 130.

Where a Sidecar is Fitted. Do not forget to lubricate the sidecar-wheel hub. According to the type of hub bearings fitted (see appropriate sidecar instructions), oil or grease the sidecar hub about every 1,000 miles when attending to the other hubs. Some other lubrication points on the sidecar chassis need greasing.

Maintenance of Front Forks (1954-66). See page 116.

Topping-up Front Forks (1947-53). It is necessary to top-up the Panther-Dowty "Oleomatic" front forks only in the event of "bottoming" occurring in spite of the forks being correctly inflated (see page 117). Absolute cleanliness must be observed during the topping-up, the procedure for which is as below.

1. Remove the dust cap from the inflation valve B (Fig. 18).
2. Depress the stem of the inflation valve and allow *all* air to escape. On doing this the fork legs will close up.
3. Support the crankcase of the engine in a manner such that both fork legs are *one inch* from the fully closed position.
4. Unscrew the two hexagon-headed filler plugs (A, Fig. 18) from the upper ends of the fork legs, and then top-up each fork leg with one of the following oils—

  (*a*) Wakefield's Castrolite.
  (*b*) Shell X-100 20/20 W.
  (*c*) Mobiloil Arctic.
  (*d*) B.P. Energol SAE 20.
  (*e*) Essolube 20.

CORRECT LUBRICATION 41

5. Fit and retighten the two filler plugs after making sure that the rubber seals are not damaged.

6. Remove the crankcase support and depress the inflation

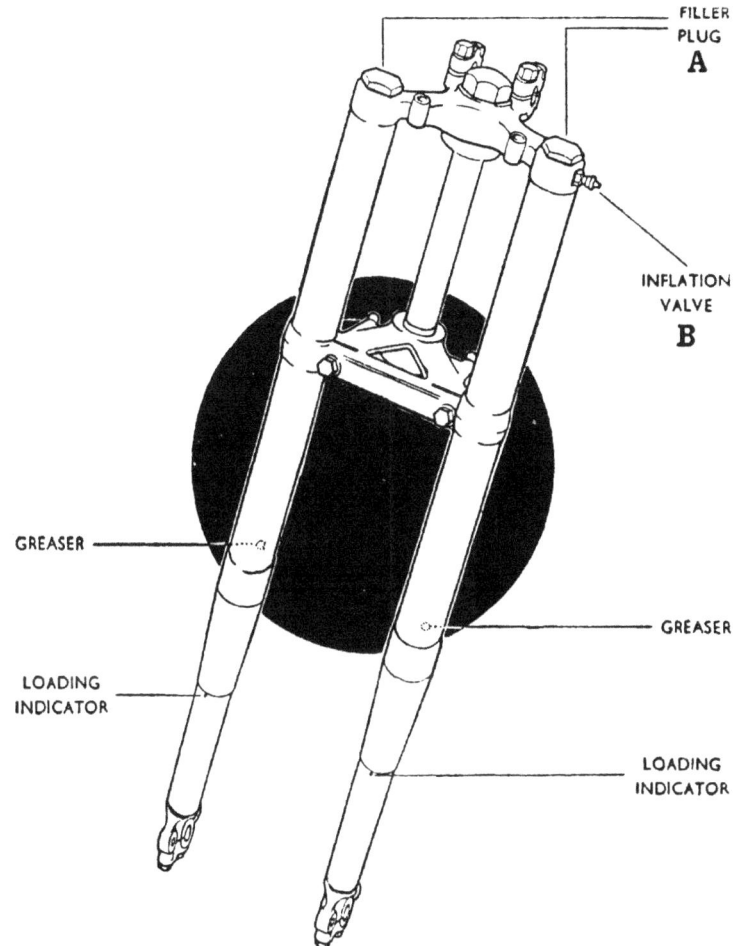

FIG. 18. PANTHER-DOWTY "OLEOMATIC" FRONT FORKS (1947-53)
Showing features concerned with lubrication and maintenance.

valve so as to allow all surplus oil to drain off and the fork legs to close completely.

7. Inflate the front forks correctly (see page 117), according to actual load, and replace the dust cap on the inflation valve.

Refilling Front Forks (1947-53). It should not be necessary to change the oil in the Panther-Dowty "Oleomatic" front forks unless (*a*) the oil has become contaminated during topping-up or filling, (*b*) the oil has for some reason been drained off completely, or (*c*) the front fork legs are dismantled. If it becomes necessary to refill the front forks, use one of the five oils mentioned previously, and follow the topping-up procedure already described. It is, of course, necessary to insert considerably more oil.

Greasing Front Forks (1947-53). Apply the grease gun about every 500 miles (or weekly) to the two greasers (see Fig. 18) located at the rear of the fork-leg outer tubes close to the lower bearings, which must be regularly greased. Grease as used for the motor-cycle parts (see page 39) is suitable. Inject about *six shots* of grease through each of the two nipples. Any surplus grease will escape through the vent holes which are provided in the sides of the outer tubes.

Greasing Front Forks (1938-46). About every 1,000 miles apply the grease gun to the nipples provided on the Panther-Webb girder-type front forks. Continue greasing until grease begins to exude from the ends of the fork spindles. Use one of the greases recommended on page 39 for the motor-cycle parts.

Lubricating Brake Operation. About every 1,000 miles grease the front and rear brake cam spindles and weekly the spindle for the rear brake pedal (see Fig. 16). At the same time apply a little oil or grease to the linkage. See also page 130.

The Control Cables and Handlebar Levers. Each week apply an oil can (engine oil) to the various handlebar levers, and do not forget to oil the exposed ends of the operating cables which are subjected to considerable stresses. Also oil the nipples.

Lubrication of Dimming Switch. About every 5,000 miles lubricate the moving parts of the switch with a little thin machine oil. A Lucas switch is fitted to all 1945 and later models.

Lubricating Speedometer Drive. About once every 3,000 miles the speedometer drive should be lubricated. This is important to prevent undue wear and to ensure accurate speedometer readings. Disconnect the flexible-drive cable and grease it thoroughly, also grease and replace the speedometer gearbox; a grease nipple is provided (see Fig. 16).

On 1938-46 Panthers with girder-type front forks the speedometer drive is taken off the front wheel, but on 1947 and later four-speed Panthers with telescopic-type front forks the drive is taken off the rear wheel hub. In both cases an accessible grease

CORRECT LUBRICATION 43

nipple is fitted to the speedometer gearbox. Any of the greases mentioned on page 39 are satisfactory for lubricating the drive and gearbox.

The Front and Rear or Centre Stands. Occasonially smear a little engine oil on the stand-pivot bolts.

Replenishing Oil Sump. On page 33 reference is made to replenishing the sump with 3-4 pints of engine oil. Note that if the entire engine has *not* been drained, three pints is sufficient. Replenish with four pints only if the timing case has been drained and the whole of the oil removed.

It is advisable not to overfill the sump, as this only increases pressure in the crankcase and, therefore, oil consumption. Although the maximum capacity of the sump is approximately four pints, if you pour this amount into the sump of a *new* engine you will observe that after a few minutes running the level drops by the equivalent of about one pint, or to groove B (see Fig. 13) on the dip-stick. The "lost" oil is retained in the timing case, the rocker-box, cylinder-head ducts, and various other oil channels. For the above reasons it is advisable always to regard groove B on the dip-stick as indicating the correct oil level unless, of course, the entire engine has been drained of oil.

Oils for Very Cold Weather. To ensure easy starting in the U.K. or overseas when the air temperature remains below 32° F., it is advisable to replenish the oil sump with one of the five oils recommended on page 40 for topping-up the Panther-Dowty front forks.

Grease Steering Head Every 3,000 Miles. About every 3,000 miles inject a small amount of grease through the nipple (see Fig. 16) provided for lubricating the steering-head bearings.

Rear Suspension. Grease the "swinging arm" pivot bearing (see Fig. 63) every 500 miles. The Armstrong-type shock-absorber units provided on most 1954-66 Panthers contain sufficient SAE 10 mineral oil for an indefinite running period, and no maintenance is necessary. The shock-absorber units, however, are quickly adjustable for load as described on pages 133-6.

CHAPTER IV
MAINTAINING A GOOD SPARK

THE maintenance of a "fat spark" at the sparking plug helps quick starting, and ensures thorough and rapid combustion of fuel, necessary to obtain maximum performance. This chapter tells you how to keep the ignition system at the peak of efficiency.

THE SPARKING PLUG

The combustion chamber is an extraordinarily hot place (sometimes around 1,500°F.). Therefore always run on a reputable make of plug of the correct type.

Suitable Plugs. All 1938 and subsequent engines require a 14 mm. sparking plug with a 12·5 mm. ($\frac{1}{2}$ in.) reach. Three excellent makes are the Lodge, K.L.G., and the Champion, and you can rely on them absolutely. For the correct types to fit see page 14.

Weatherproof Plug Terminals. Those who ride in all weather conditions are advised to fit a weatherproof terminal cover to the sparking plug. Excellent and cheap waterproof terminal covers are available for K.L.G., Lodge, and Champion sparking plugs. A typical example is shown in Fig. 19. All three types of terminal covers are extremely easy to fit to the existing H.T. lead and completely cover the terminal and top insulation of the sparking plug.

Effect of Faulty Plug. If no spark occurs, the engine will refuse to start, or if started will stop. If the plug fires irregularly, there will ensue one or more of the following: difficult starting, irregular slow-running, and some intermittent misfiring, accompanied perhaps by some "banging" in the exhaust system.

Testing a Plug. A rough and ready method of testing a plug is to lay it on the cylinder head with the terminal clear of the head; then rotate the engine smartly with the kick-starter and see whether the plug sparks well and regularly. A series of distinct "clicks" should be audible. A garage method of testing is to apply a pencil-type neon tube tester to the plug terminal with the engine running.

If the sparking plug sparks weakly or fails to spark while

MAINTAINING A GOOD SPARK

satisfactory sparks occur at the end of the h.t. lead (see page 53), carefully inspect and attend to the plug, if still serviceable

Inspecting Sparking Plug. Before scrapping a faulty plug, scrutinize it closely. If the electrodes are badly burned, the plug should be placed in the dustbin. Bad burning in an unreasonably short time suggests too small a plug gap or an incorrect mixture.

Light-coloured fuel deposits do not appreciably affect efficiency

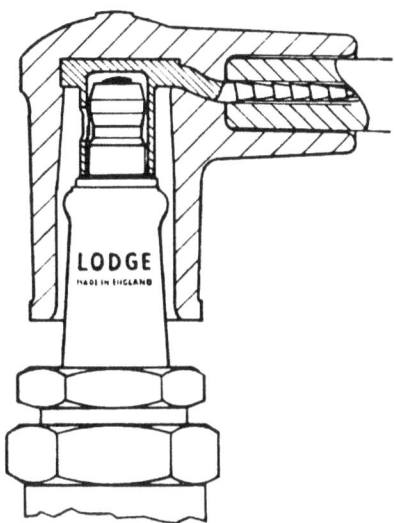

FIG. 19. LODGE WEATHERPROOF TERMINAL COVER

unless accompanied by oiling-up or a generally bad condition of the plug. They should, however, be removed. Inspect the plug carefully for carbon deposits which are highly detrimental and must be completely removed by cleaning the plug thoroughly.

Carbon deposits are caused by mixture fouling, and also by oil fouling. In the former case the deposits are *dull black* and sooty. In the latter instance they are generally *shiny black*, hard, and moist. If rapid fouling occurs, the nature of the deposits often gives a clue as to how they may be reduced.

Inspect for Oiling-up. Examine the sparking plug for oiling-up, often present with carbon deposits. The plug when oiled-up is dirty and moist with engine oil. The remedy is careful cleaning.

During running-in (see page 15) some oiling-up is inevitable, but subsequently a tendency for persistent oiling-up generally indicates excessive oil pressure (see page 31), badly fitted or worn piston rings, or a worn cylinder and/or piston.

The Plug Insulation. Verify that the sparking plug insulation is not slightly cracked or seriously damaged, and that it is clean (internally and externally).

The Washer. Check that the copper washer (between the plug body and the cylinder head) is undamaged. Scrap it if its condition causes compression leakage or "blowing" (evidenced by

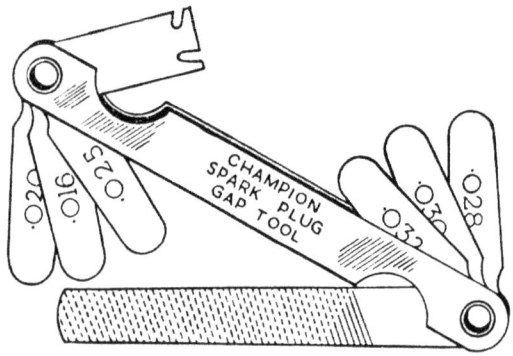

FIG. 20. AN EXTREMELY USEFUL CHAMPION TOOL

This sparking plug maintenance tool has, as may be observed, a slotted blade for adjusting the earth electrode(s), six feeler gauges for checking the plug gap, and a fine file for brightening up the plug electrode points. It should be included in your tool kit.

blackening), or if the washer has become flattened and hard, thus reducing heat conductivity.

Checking the Plug Gap. On removing the sparking plug for inspection and cleaning, always check the gap between the electrodes (points). The sparking plug gap must be maintained correct at 0·025 in. An incorrect gap tends to make starting difficult, causes misfiring, and spoils the general performance of the engine. Too small a gap increases any tendency for oiling-up to occur; an excessively wide gap, besides causing overheating of the centre electrode (thereby increasing the risk of pre-ignition), is liable to impose a dangerous stress on the windings of the magneto, and cause difficult starting.

The terrific heat of combustion and the sparks cause the points to burn gradually away, thereby increasing the gap. Therefore, about every 2,500 miles (and when ignition trouble occurs) remove the plug and check its gap with a suitable feeler

MAINTAINING A GOOD SPARK

gauge, obtainable from accessory firms (see Fig. 20) or the plug manufacturers.*

Insert the blade of the feeler gauge between the centre (insulated) electrode and the outer electrode(s). If the plug gap is appreciably more or less than 0·025 in., re-gap the plug immediately, *after* first making sure that the points are quite clean. *Note:* a fairly wide gap gives a better spark.

Re-gapping Sparking Plug. If the gap between the plug electrodes exceeds or is less than 0·025 in., re-gap it by *pressing* inwards the *outer* electrode(s). Do not attempt to tap the outer electrode(s), and *never* exert any pressure on the centre electrode. If you are using a single-point sparking plug, re-gapping is best done with a tool of the type shown in Fig. 20. A Lodge set of feeler gauges and combined re-gapping tool is also available.

Clean the Sparking Plug Frequently. Remove the plug frequently and clean it. It is not necessary to take the plug to bits every time you clean it. If the plug is not very dirty, brighten up the electrode points with a points file or some fine emery cloth. Clean the plug body with a wire-brush cleaner.

An excellent proprietary plug cleaner (obtainable from accessory firms) consists of a metal reservoir containing loose steel wires and petrol. To remove superficial carbon deposits, screw the sparking plug into the reservoir and vigorously shake it.

About every 2,500-3,000 miles (and when plug trouble occurs) remove the sparking plug and clean it very thoroughly internally and externally. If the plug is of the detachable type dismantle the plug first. Champion L-7 plugs cannot be dismantled. When cleaning a plug quickly, wipe the outside with a cloth moistened with petrol. Much-used plugs are difficult to dismantle.

To Clean Lodge or K.L.G. Plug Thoroughly. Fig. 21 shows a typical detachable-type sparking plug (K.L.G.) dismantled for thorough cleaning. To dismantle a detachable-type plug, hold the larger hexagon of the plug body D lightly in a vice or with a suitable spanner. If using a vice, be very careful not to *squeeze* the hexagon. Next with the plug box spanner (shown at 11 in Fig. 39) applied to the smaller hexagon of the gland nut B, unscrew the gland nut until it is separated from the plug body. The centre electrode F with its insulation (comprising the insulated electrode

---

* The makers of Lodge, Champion, and K.L.G. sparking plugs are: Lodge Plugs, Ltd., Rugby; Champion Sparking Plug Co., Ltd., Feltham, Middlesex; and Smith's Motor Accessories, Ltd., Cricklewood Works, London, N.W.2.

assembly A) can then be detached from the gland nut. Be careful not to lose the internal washer H.

To clean the insulation, first wash it (if oily) in petrol or paraffin. Next with fairly coarse glass-paper, remove all carbon deposits

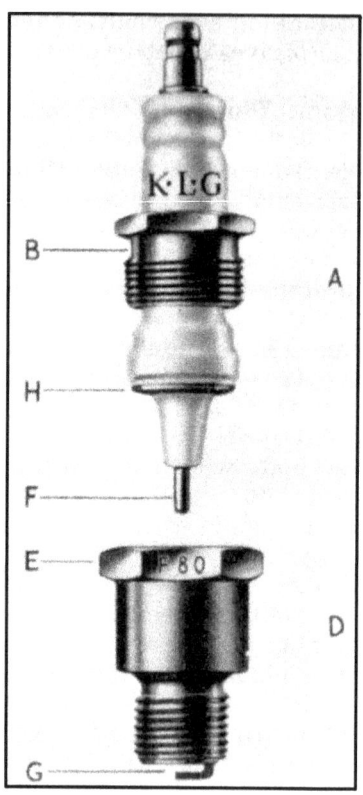

Fig. 21. Detachable Type Sparking Plug (K.L.G.) Dismantled for thorough Cleaning

In the illustration the gland nut B and the internal washer H have not been removed from the insulation.

and again wash in petrol or paraffin. On no account scrape the insulation with a knife.

To clean the metal parts (body and gland nut), use a small knife or a wire brush. Scrape the inside of the plug body D, and the earthed electrode(s) G quite clean. Afterwards rinse the parts in petrol. The gland nut seldom gets very dirty, but there may be considerable carbon deposits inside the plug body and also on the external threads. Clean and polish the points of the centre and earthed electrodes F and G with some *fine* emery cloth.

MAINTAINING A GOOD SPARK

When assembling the plug, see that there is no dirt or grit lodged between the body of the plug and the insulation of the centre electrode. Smear a little *thin* oil on the internal washer and make sure that the washer seats properly, to ensure a gas-tight seal. Avoid excessive tightening of the gland nut B. Finally verify that the gap is correct (see page 46).

To Clean Champion Plug Thoroughly. A Champion non-detachable plug such as the L-7 cannot be dismantled and cleaned like the detachable Lodge and K.L.G. plugs. Quick cleaning is, of course, done in the same manner (see page 47). The best method of cleaning a Champion plug thoroughly is to take it to a nearby garage having a suitable service unit. In a matter of a few minutes the plug can be thoroughly cleaned of all deposits, washed, subjected to a high-pressure air line, and subsequently tested for sparking at a pressure exceeding 100 lb. per sq. in. Lodge and K.L.G. plugs can be similarly dealt with.

Replacing the Sparking Plug. Before doing this, clean the threads with a wire brush, as carbon is a bad conductor. Also verify that the external copper washer is sound (see page 46). Do not employ excessive force with the box spanner when replacing the plug. Check that the h.t. lead is firmly secured to the plug terminal and the h.t. pick-up.

MAGNETO MAINTENANCE (1938-66)

The 14 mm. plug is "sparked" by a generator mounted above the crankcase behind the cylinder and driven by a gear meshing with the gear whose boss houses the oil-pump plunger. This section covers the maintenance of the four different instruments used on 1938 and subsequent Panthers.

Lubrication Instructions. Advice on lubrication is given in Chapter III, and the appropriate instructions should be closely observed. The magneto drive is automatically lubricated, being enclosed in the timing case.

Check Contact-breaker Gap. If the magneto or contact-breaker is quite new, some initial bedding-down occurs and it is advisable to check the gap between the contacts after the first 100 miles and again when 500 miles have been covered. Thereafter check the contact-breaker gap about every 3,000 miles. Always maintain the gap at 0·012 in. where a Lucas or B.T.H. magneto or Lucas "Magdyno" is fitted, and at 0·015-0·018 in. in the case of a Miller "Dyno-mag."

Failure to maintain the contact-breaker gap within the permitted limits will adversely affect the ignition, and may alter the timing to a small extent. To check and adjust the gap, use the following procedure—

1. Take off the contact-breaker cover and turn the engine slowly forwards until the contacts open fully (just after top dead centre on the firing stroke).

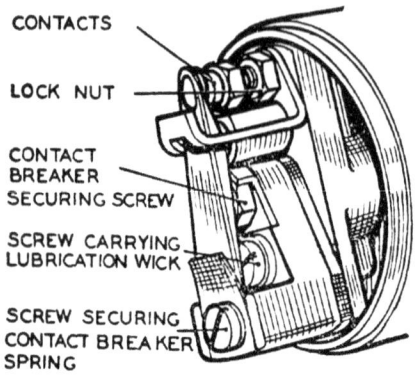

FIG. 22. FACE-CAM CONTACT-BREAKER ON LUCAS N1 MAGNETO OR "MAGDYNO".
Applies to all 1945 and subsequent models.

2. Slide the blade of the feeler gauge (attached to the magneto spanner) between the contacts. If the blade just enters without friction, the gap is correct, and no adjustment is required. But if the blade is a loose fit, or it is necessary to spring the contacts to allow it to enter, the contact-breaker gap needs adjusting.

To Adjust Gap (Lucas N1 Magneto or "Magdyno"). On 1945-51 models provided with a Lucas type N1 magneto and on late 1951 and subsequent models with a Lucas "Magdyno," adjust the contact-breaker gap, by slackening the nut which secures the fixed-contact screw (see Fig. 22) and then turning this screw by its hexagon head until the correct gap between the fixed and movable contacts is obtained. Afterwards firmly retighten the lock-nut and again check the gap. If correct, replace the contact-breaker cover.

To Adjust Gap (B.T.H. Magneto). The "K" type B.T.H. magneto fitted to 1938 Panthers has a contact-breaker as shown in Fig. 23. This contact-breaker (not of the face-cam type) incorporates a rocker arm with fibre heel bearing on a cam ring.

To adjust the gap between the contacts on the B.T.H. contact-breaker, loosen the lock-nut A and then turn the contact screw fixed to the rocker arm with the magneto spanner applied to the hexagon B until the gap is found to be correct. Tighten lock-nut A and again check the gap. On this particular contact-breaker the contacts have slightly

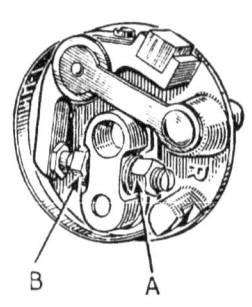

FIG. 23. CONTACT-BREAKER ON B.T.H. MAGNETO
Applies to 1938 models only.

MAINTAINING A GOOD SPARK

convex surfaces, and this should be borne in mind when checking the gap.

To Adjust Gap (Miller "Dyno-mag"). To adjust the gap between the contacts of the Miller "Dyno-mag" fitted to 1939-40 models, first rotate the magneto armature until the adjustable contact and nut are opposite the enlarged portion of the cam. Then with the magneto spanner loosen the lock-nut and turn the adjustable-contact screw until the correct gap is obtained. Retighten the lock-nut and again check the gap.

Keep Contact-breaker Clean. Never allow the contact-breaker, and especially the contacts, to become dirty, oily, or pitted, otherwise you will encounter serious ignition trouble. Burned and pitted contact faces are generally the result of an incorrect gap and/or dirty contacts.

Always inspect the contacts when checking the contact-breaker gap. If cleaning is necessary, do this *before* making a final adjustment of the gap. A *grey, smooth* appearance of the contacts indicates that they are in good condition, and are best left well alone.

Slightly discoloured contacts can generally be cleaned up satisfactorily by wiping them with a cloth moistened with petrol. If Lucas or Miller contacts are found to be blackened or badly pitted, clean them with a slip of fine carborundum if available, or if not, with some *fine* emery cloth. On the B.T.H. magneto fitted to 1938 Panthers, only the use of fine emery cloth is permissible, because of the slightly convex shape of the contacts (some Lucas contacts are also convex). After cleaning the contacts remove *all* metallic dust and dirt with a petrol-moistened cloth.

During the cleaning and truing-up of the contacts be very careful not to remove more than the barest amount of contact metal that is needed to ensure: (*a*) brightness of the surfaces, (*b*) parallelism of the two contacts, and (*c*) true faces having absolute smoothness. To obtain the best results, partial or complete removal of the contact-breaker is desirable for pitted contacts.

In the case of the Lucas type N1 magneto (1945-51) or Lucas "Magdyno" (late 1951 onwards) the contacts can be effectively cleaned after removing the spring arm (see Fig. 22) carrying the moving contact. To remove the spring arm it is only necessary to remove the fixing screw and the spring washer behind it. Be sure when replacing the spring arm to fit the small backing spring in its original position (with the curved portion facing *outwards* as shown in Fig. 22). See that the contacts meet squarely. At long intervals check the contact-breaker tappet for wear.

The contact-breaker of the B.T.H. type "K" magneto (1938

models) can be readily removed for cleaning. Unscrew the central hexagon-headed screw and remove the complete contact-breaker. Then lift the contact lever by first raising and then moving to one side the check spring which is located in the end of the bearing bush. Be careful not to distort the contact-lever control spring.

Before replacing the B.T.H. contact lever, smear the bearing bush with a little thin oil (see page 34). See that all surplus oil is wiped off to prevent any getting on the contacts. Clean the back plate and see that the contact-breaker is replaced so that it fits properly into the keyed recess of the armature.

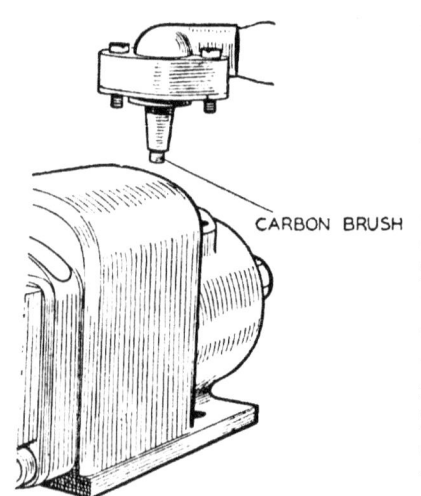

FIG. 24. THE H.T. PICK-UP REMOVED FROM LUCAS N1 MAGNETO (1945-51)

On late 1951 models onwards with the Lucas "Magdyno" the pick-up is similar.

Where a Miller "Dyno-mag" is fitted (1939-40 models) it is also advisable about every 10,000 miles to remove the complete contact-breaker for thorough cleaning and dressing of the contacts. To do this it is only necessary to unscrew the centre fixing bolt. When replacing the contact-breaker, make sure that the tongue on the centre hole of the contact-breaker engages the key-way on the shaft. Keep the contact-breaker cover clean and dry.

The Magneto or "Magdyno" Slip-ring. Moisture, oil, or carbon deposits collecting on the slip-ring of the instrument are liable to cause difficulty in starting, and misfiring. It is therefore advisable periodically (say, once every 4,000 miles) to remove the two screws holding the h.t. pick-up to the instrument (see Fig. 24) and clean the slip-ring track and flanges thoroughly. Insert through the exposed aperture a clean soft cloth so that it bears against the slip-ring while slowly rotating the engine. The cloth may be wrapped round a pencil, but on no account must any implement be used in such a manner as to exert undue pressure on the slip-ring flanges, which are readily damaged.

The H.T. Pick-up. When cleaning the slip-ring, clean also the surface of the pick-up moulding with a cloth moistened with petrol, and polish with a fine dry cloth. Inspect the pick-up moulding for cracks, and closely examine the carbon brush and spring.

MAINTAINING A GOOD SPARK

The carbon brush (see Fig. 24) must be able to move freely in its holder, but when examining it, be careful not to stretch the brush spring unduly. Renew the brush at once if badly worn. Also renew the spring if this has weakened.

When replacing the h.t. pick-up, do not forget to replace the small gasket between the pick-up and the body of the magneto or "Magdyno."

Renewing Pick-up Cable (Lucas Magneto or "Magdyno"). On 1945 and later Panthers with a Lucas magneto or "Magdyno," to renew a perished or cracked h.t. cable, always use 7 mm. rubber-covered ignition cable. Bare the end of the cable (see Fig. 25) for about ¼ in. and thread the cable through the moulded terminal. Thread the wire through the metal washer and then bend back the cable strands, as shown in Fig. 25. Finally screw the moulded terminal into the pick-up moulding.

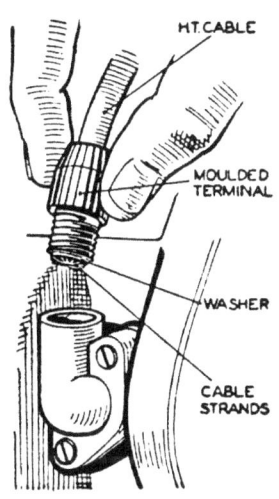

FIG. 25. RENEWING LUCAS H.T. PICK-UP CABLE

Testing for Spark at H.T. Lead. To test for sparking at the plug end of the h.t. lead, kick the engine over smartly while the h.t. lead is held close to one of the cylinder fins. Alternatively without detaching the lead from the sparking plug, place the steel blade of a wooden-handled screwdriver with part of the blade in contact with the plug terminal and another part of the blade almost in contact with a cylinder fin. When the engine is rotated smartly, "fat" sparks should occur regularly.

Lucas Automatic Ignition-timing Unit. This is provided on 1947-9 and early 1950 models fitted with Lucas N1 magnetos. The unit is inside the engine timing-case, and normally requires no attention. But sometimes after a very big mileage it may be desirable to renew the two springs (see Fig. 26). If such renewal is required, it is essential to obtain genuine Lucas springs, graduated for Panther engines.

How the Unit Works. With the engine, and therefore the Lucas magneto, stationary, the movable weights are in the closed position and the magneto is automatically *retarded* for starting purposes. When the engine is accelerated the movable weights by centrifugal force extend the springs and the weights move outwards, thus causing the shaft driving the Lucas magneto to move relatively to the driving gear, and advancing the ignition timing accordingly. The maximum advance obtainable is 38° before top dead centre (T.D.C.), measured in degrees of crankshaft rotation.

Magneto Removal and Ignition Timing. Note that on all 1938–40 and subsequent models the magneto, "Dyno-mag," or "Magdyno" can be removed *without* disturbing the ignition timing if both the coupling dogs are marked before removal and replaced in exactly the same positions.

The Lucas "Magdyno" (used on 1951–7 models) has an Oldham

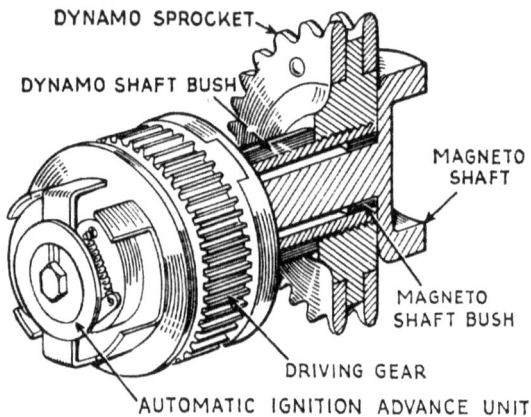

FIG. 26. DETAILS OF LUCAS AUTOMATIC IGNITION-TIMING UNIT

Fitted to 1947–9 and early 1950 models.

type fibre coupling and the "Magdyno" is secured in position by steel straps. Do not remove these straps from the crankcase or loosen their fixing screws, otherwise the drive will become misaligned.

Before Checking or Re-setting Ignition Timing. Always check that the gap between the contacts of the contact-breaker is correct (see page 49), otherwise an exact timing will *not* be obtainable. Take up slackness in the timing control.

Timing Ignition (1947–50 Models). On 1947–50 models with the automatic timing, if the magneto driving sprocket is removed, retiming is extremely simple. The following on all models is the procedure to use.

It is assumed that the contact-breaker and timing case covers

MAINTAINING A GOOD SPARK

are removed. With the magneto driving-gear in mesh, but with the sleeve nut and withdrawing device (Fig. 27) loosened so that the driving gear and automatic ignition timing unit are free to move relatively to the magneto-drive shaft, turn the contact-breaker until the contacts are just beginning to open with the piston at T.D.C. on the *compression* stroke, and with the ignition fully retarded (outwards). The automatic timing unit does, of

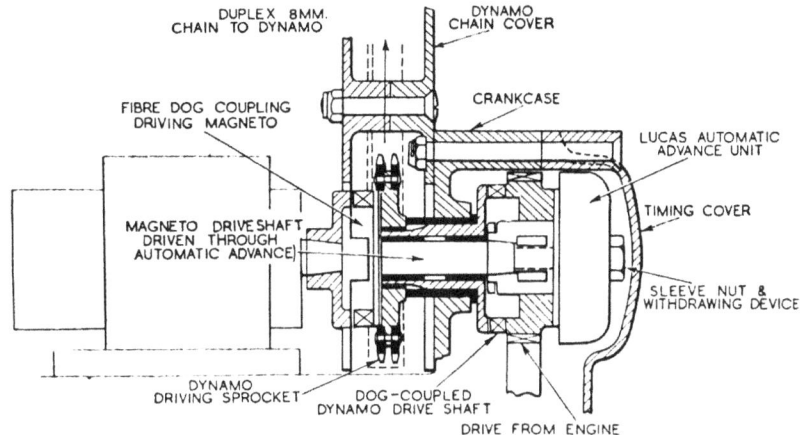

FIG. 27. SECTIONAL DRAWING OF LUCAS MAGNETO AND DYNAMO DRIVE (1947-50)

On late 1950-66 "Magdyno" models the automatic ignition-timing unit is omitted.

(*By courtesy of "Motor Cycle," London*)

course, keep the ignition in the fully retarded position when the engine is stationary.

To determine the exact moment of the contact-breaker "break," insert a cellophane slip between the contacts of the contact-breaker and exert a gentle pull on the cellophane when the contacts are about to open.

To obtain the true T.D.C. position of the piston, remove the sparking plug and slip a $\frac{1}{4}$ in. diameter rod (or a round pencil) through the plug hole and then rotate the engine slowly forwards until it is *felt* that the piston is exactly at the top of its stroke after the resistance of compression is met or it has been ascertained that both valves are fully closed.* See that you do not time on

* With the sparking plug fitted, and the decompressor out of action, stiff engine compression can be felt as the piston approaches T.D.C., when the engine is slowly rotated, but if there is any doubt about T.D.C. being on the compression stroke, raise the lower portion of the push-rod cover tube (see page 82) and observe whether both tappets are fully closed.

the exhaust stroke. When the piston is at true T.D.C. no movement is imparted to the rod when "rocking" the engine slightly.

After precisely determining the piston T.D.C. position and magneto "break," retighten the sleeve nut and withdrawing device (see Fig. 27) and again check that the contacts begin to open with the piston at T.D.C. (equivalent to approximately 38° before T.D.C. on full-advance). Finally replace the contact-breaker and timing-case covers, not forgetting the paper washer for the timing-case cover.

Timing Ignition (1950 Models Onwards). On Lucas magneto or "Magdyno" (1951-6) models with manual ignition-control the foregoing instructions for Lucas magneto-ignition models are applicable, but note that after finding true T.D.C. on the compression stroke you must turn the engine *backwards* until the piston has descended (approximately $\frac{7}{16}$ in., or 33° before T.D.C.), using the indicator rod method referred to later for the 1938-40 models. With the ignition lever *fully advanced*, and the piston $\frac{7}{16}$ in. before T.D.C., set the contact-breaker so that the contacts are beginning to open, and lock the driving-gear. The timing should then be correct. Check again to make sure.

Timing Ignition (1938-40 Models). On 1938-40 Panthers with B.T.H. magneto (1938) or Miller "Dyno-mag" (1939-40) manual ignition-control is provided, and the procedure for retiming the ignition in the event of the magneto driving-gear being removed, is as follows.

Remove the magneto or "Dyno-mag" from the crankcase and slacken off the driving dog on the tapered armature-shaft extension. Now replace the magneto or "Dyno-mag" and after moving the ignition lever on the near side of the handlebars to the maximum advance position (fully *inwards*) and setting the piston at $\frac{19}{32}$ in. (45 deg.) before T.D.C. on the *compression* stroke, set the magneto or "Dyno-mag" so that its contacts *just* begin to open.

To set the piston in the correct position, first find the true T.D.C. position already described for timing the ignition on 1947-50 Model 100 engines. Then to obtain the required $\frac{19}{32}$ in. advance before T.D.C., mark the indicator rod (or pencil) inserted through the sparking-plug hole, flush with the top of the body of an old sparking-plug screwed into the cylinder head.

Remove the indicator rod and scratch another mark on it exactly $\frac{19}{32}$ in. *above* the first mark. After again inserting the rod, slowly turn the engine backwards by means of the rear wheel (with a gear engaged) until the upper of the two marks on the rod

MAINTAINING A GOOD SPARK

is flush with the top of the sparking-plug body. The piston has now, of course, descended so that it is exactly at $1\frac{9}{32}$ in. before T.D.C. A degree disc can be attached to the crankshaft to indicate 45 deg. before T.D.C. and this gives very accurate timing, but for all normal purposes a measurement taken on the piston stroke is quite sufficiently accurate.

To obtain the precise moment of the magneto or "Dyno-mag" contact "break," use a slip of cellophane (see page 55).

After setting the magneto or "Dyno-mag" to give the correct timing, mark the positions of the dog and fibre coupling, remove the magneto or "Dyno-mag" and firmly tighten the nut securing its driving dog. When tightening this nut be very careful not to permit the driving dog to move the slightest amount on the armature shaft taper. Finally replace the magneto or "Dyno-mag" on the engine crankcase with the driving dog and fibre coupling marks exactly coinciding. The ignition timing must then be correct, but it is advisable to check the timing again, before replacing the contact-breaker cover and sparking plug, in case the driving dog should have moved while its securing nut was being tightened.

CHAPTER V

THE LIGHTING SET

To ensure pleasant and safe night riding, always give your lighting set the little but regular attention which it needs. This chapter deals with dynamo, battery, and lamp maintenance. The ignition portion of the Lucas "Magdyno" (1951 onwards) or Miller "Dyno-mag" (1939-40) has already been dealt with.

DYNAMO MAINTENANCE

The following dynamo maintenance instructions apply, except where otherwise stated, to 1945-9 E3H and 1950-66 E3LM 36-watt Lucas dynamos (fitted separately or on Lucas "Magdynos"), and also to the 1939-44 Miller "Dyno-mags" and to Miller dynamos used on 1933 Panthers.

To Avoid Accidental " Shortings." Precautions are unnecessary for inspecting the dynamo commutator, but on making any adjustments to the wiring circuit or removing the lighting switch from the headlamp, always take some steps to prevent accidental "shorting," i.e. disconnect the lead from the ammeter B terminal to the battery positive (negative, 1952 onwards) terminal.

Unscrew the terminal (1954 onwards) or push back the rubber shield and unscrew the brass cable-connector at the battery. When doing this be sure that the cable does not make contact with any metal parts of the frame. When reconnecting the lead, pull the rubber shield well over the connector.

Servicing. It is a good plan every 10,000-15,000 miles to entrust the dynamo, "Dyno-mag," or "Magdyno" to a service depot or agent for dismantling, cleaning, lubrication, and general servicing.

Inspect Commutator and Brushgear Every 5,000-6,000 Miles. The Lucas or Miller dynamo will run satisfactorily for thousands of miles with scarcely any attention other than occasional inspection of the commutator and brushgear. It is advisable every 5,000-6,000 miles, to remove the metal cover-band from the dynamo and make a careful inspection.

The Commutator Brushes. The brushes of the Lucas or Miller dynamo must be absolutely clean and able to move freely in their box-type holders, on holding back the retaining springs and gently

THE LIGHTING SET

pulling on the leads and then releasing them. There must also be perfect and firm contact between the brushes and the copper segments of the commutator; the brush faces in contact with the segments should be uniformly polished.

Clean the brushes with a petrol-moistened cloth after removing them. To do this, pull back each brush-retaining spring (see Fig. 28) and remove the brush by pulling on its lead, being careful to see that the brush pressure-spring is clear of the brush holder. See that the spring is not distorted, or it will be unable to exert its full pressure on the brush when the brush wears down, and irregular charging will ensue.

Examine the carbon brushes for wear and unevenness; true them up if necessary. Generally it is best to renew the brushes *before* serious wear develops, as this prevents sparking, which causes blackening of the commutator and an unsteady charging current. Always replace serviceable brushes in their *original* positions.

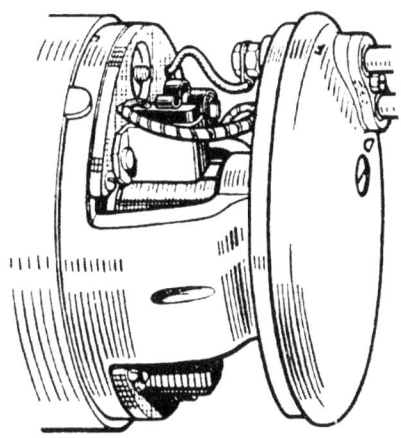

FIG. 28. COMMUTATOR END OF LUCAS E3LM DYNAMO (1950-66)

The metal cover-band is shown removed. The E3H dynamo fitted to 1945-9 Panthers is very similar, but a lubricator is fitted to the commutator driving-end bracket.

If Lucas or Miller brushes become so badly worn that it is necessary to renew them, this can easily be done as follows: Release the eyelet on the brush lead by unscrewing the hexagonal nut or screw at the terminal; then, holding back the spring lever out of the way, withdraw the brush from its holder. Renew, always, with brushes of the same make as the instrument itself.

The brush springs should be inspected occasionally, to see that they have sufficient tension to keep the brushes firmly in contact with the commutator when the dynamo is running. It is particularly necessary to bear this in mind when the brushes have been in use a long time and are very much worn down.

It is unwise to insert brushes of a grade other than that normally supplied for the dynamo, or to change the tension springs. The arrangement provided has been made only after many years of experience, and will be found to give the best results and the longest life.

When commutator brushes have become so worn that they no longer bed down properly on the commutator, it is best to have new brushes fitted and bedded by a service depot or agent.

The Commutator Segments. The surface of the commutator segments must be kept clean and free from oil or brush dust, etc. If any grease or oil gains access to the commutator through over-lubrication, it will not only cause sparking, but in addition carbon and copper dust will collect in the grooves between the segments and cause trouble.

The best way to clean the commutator without disconnecting any leads is to remove from its box-holder one of the main brushes and, inserting a fine dry cloth, hold it with a suitably-shaped piece of wood, against the commutator surface, causing the armature to be rotated* at the same time. If the commutator is very dirty, moisten the cloth with petrol. If it has been neglected for long periods, it may need cleaning with fine glasspaper, but this needs armature removal, and should not be necessary if it has received regular attention. The segments should be *dark bronze* in colour and highly polished.

Keep the Dynamo Chain Tension Correct. Check the tension of a separate dynamo chain at regular intervals, and particularly during the first few thousand miles when some initial stretch often occurs. Should the dynamo chain be too slack, there is a risk of the chain jumping off the sprockets and causing damage. If the chain is too taut, a severe stress is imposed on the armature shaft driving bearings. On 1947-9 and early 1950 models this stress also results in a sluggish action of the Lucas automatic ignition-timing unit provided.

To check the tension of the duplex driving-chain insert the fingers through the hole in the rear of the chain cover. Check the tension at several points on the chain run. With the dynamo chain correctly tensioned, there should be about $\frac{1}{8}$ in. (total) up and down movement possible on fully deflecting the chain with the fingers.

The Lucas or Miller (1938 models) dynamo is mounted eccentrically to its casing to provide an adjustment for chain tension. To adjust the tension of the dynamo chain, loosen the nut securing the clinch band and rotate the dynamo bodily as required to obtain the required $\frac{1}{8}$ in. chain whip. After retensioning the dynamo chain, make sure that you firmly retighten the nut securing the clinch band.

Compensated Voltage Control (C.V.C.). All 1939 and later Panthers incorporate compensated-voltage-control. The C.V.C. unit consists of a cut-out and voltage regulator unit neatly housed in a box beneath the saddle. The unit is connected between the

---

* To rotate the dynamo armature, slowly turn over the engine with the kick-starter, after first removing the sparking plug.

dynamo and battery and sees to it that the battery is automatically charged the right amount by varying the output of the dynamo according to the state of charge of the battery and the load imposed on it.

Current is prevented from flowing back from the battery to the dynamo at low r.p.m. by the cut-out opening. As soon as the r.p.m. rise high enough to enable the dynamo to charge the battery the cut-out closes and completes the circuit.

In all three lighting-switch positions (see page 66) the dynamo gives a controlled output and thus effects automatic charging. The Lucas regulator begins to operate when the dynamo voltage reaches about 7·3 volts. During daylight running with the battery well charged and the switch in the "Off" position the dynamo gives only a trickle charge, and the ammeter reading is unlikely to exceed 1-2 amps. Over-charging is impossible.

The regulator increases dynamo output as soon as the lamps are switched on. The effect of this after a long run with the battery voltage high, is often to show a temporary discharge reading on the ammeter, but the voltage falls fairly soon and the regulator responds, thereby causing the output of the dynamo to balance the load of the lamps.

When the battery is in a discharged state, the regulator increases the dynamo output and restores the battery to its normal state of charge in the shortest possible time.

C.V.C. Unit Needs No Adjustment. The unit is sealed by the makers, as it needs no adjustment once it is correctly set. The only conceivable trouble is oxidizing or welding together of the cut-out contacts, caused by accidental crossing of the dynamo field, and positive leads. Be careful if making alterations to the wiring. Referring to Fig. 29, make sure that the C.V.C. unit connexions are correct, tight, and that the insulation is quite sound.

In the event of your fitting a Lucas "Nife" battery in place of the lead-acid type, you must fit a new regulator to ensure a good charging rate with a discharged battery. You are advised to have the change-over made at a service depot or by an agent.

Miller Dynamo (Third-brush Control). The required amount of charging by the Miller DM3G dynamo (1938 models) varies considerably according to running conditions. If the light is poor and falls off when the machine is standing, immediately charge. It is, of course, difficult to give precise charging instructions because so much depends on how often the lamps are used. The following may serve as a rough guide.

Leave the lighting switch in the *CH* (charge) position for about 1 to 1½ hours daily when undertaking much night riding. Charging a battery after discharge raises the specific gravity. Place on charge immediately, either by running the machine with the lamps off, or by using an independent source of electrical supply, any battery whose specific gravity has fallen as low as

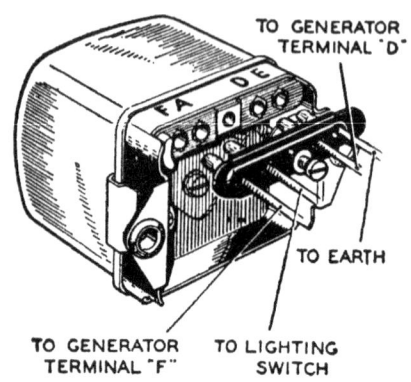

FIG. 29. CONNEXIONS ON LUCAS RB109 CUT-OUT AND REGULATOR UNIT (1958-66)
On 1938-57 Panthers the conexion sequence is F.A.D.E.

1·140. Take hydrometer readings whenever any trouble is experienced with any part of the electrical system (see page 63).

BATTERY MAINTENANCE

The battery supplies current for the front and rear lamps, and also for the electric horn. Its correct maintenance is therefore *vitally* important. This section covers the Lucas 13 amp-hour lead-acid type battery fitted to 1945 and later Panthers, and also the Exide battery provided on 1938-40 models with Miller lighting equipment.

Topping-up Battery Cells. Inspect the acid level about every *two weeks*, and more frequently in very warm weather. To inspect the electrolyte level (see Fig. 30) it is not essential actually to remove the battery. You can lift it partly out on the off side without disturbing the wiring. On all 1938 and later Panthers first slacken off the near-side fixing bolt and remove the off-side bolt. Then take off the battery lid and remove the vent plugs.

THE LIGHTING SET

Examine the hole in each vent plug and see that it is not obstructed. A choked hole will increase the pressure inside the cell because of "gassing," and may cause trouble.

Wipe the top of the battery clean and also verify that the rubber washer beneath each vent plug (if fitted) is in position. After wiping the top of the battery, either wash the rag very thoroughly, or destroy it.

Be careful not to hold a naked light near the vents. If the level of the electrolyte is below the top edges of the separators, add *distilled* water* as required to bring the level correct (see Fig. 30). *Never use tap water.* Topping-up should be done just before a charge run, as the agitation due to running and the consequent gassing will thoroughly mix the solution. A convenient device for topping-up is the Lucas battery filler. Do not add acid to the electrolyte unless some of the solution has been spilled. If this has occurred, dilute sulphuric acid of the same specific gravity as that in the cells should be added by someone experienced in the handling of batteries.

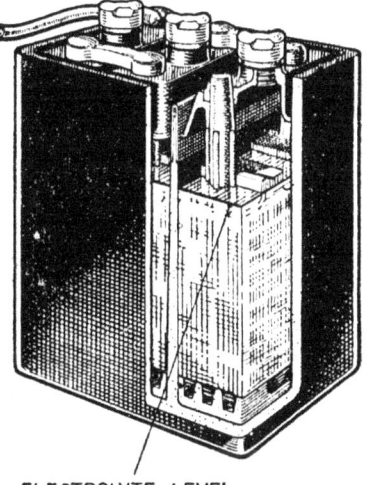

FIG. 30. KEEP THE ELECTROLYTE LEVEL WITH THE TOPS OF THE SEPARATORS

Above is shown an early type Lucas battery.

Checking Specific Gravity. Very occasionally, hydrometer readings (specific-gravity values) should be taken of the solution in each of the cells. The method of doing this with a Lucas hydrometer (battery removed) is shown in Fig. 31. The hydrometer contains a graduated float which indicates the specific gravity of the battery cell from which a sample of electrolyte is taken.

An Exide hydrometer of rather similar design to the Lucas type is made by the Chloride Electrical Storage Co., Ltd. (Exide Works, Clifton Junction, Nr. Manchester) for checking the S.G. of the electrolyte in Exide battery cells. Like the Lucas hydrometer (made by Joseph Lucas, Ltd., Birmingham, 19), it can be obtained from the makers, a service depot, or a general accessory firm (see page 79).

* Distilled water, and not the acid, is gradually lost by evaporation. Bottles of distilled water can be obtained cheaply from most garages and chemists. Some Lucas batteries have an acid-level device.

After a sample of electrolyte has been taken and checked, it must, of course, be returned to the cell concerned. The taking of S.G. readings with a hydrometer is the most efficient way of ascertaining the state of charge of the battery.

The S.G. readings should be approximately the *same for all three cells*. Should the reading for one cell differ substantially

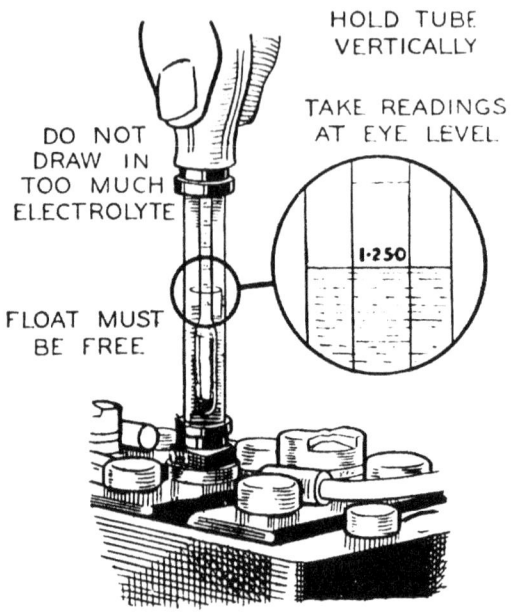

Fig. 31. Checking Specific Gravity of the Electrolyte with Lucas Hydrometer

from the readings for the others, probably some acid has been spilled or has leaked from the cell concerned. There is also a possibility of a short-circuit between the battery plates. In the latter case it will be necessary to return the battery to a service depot, agent, or other expert for attention.

Under no circumstances must the battery be allowed to remain in a discharged condition for long, or serious deterioration will inevitably occur. After checking the S.G. readings and topping-up the cells, wipe the top of the battery clean and remove any spilled electrolyte or water. Replace the vent plugs and the battery lid. Then fit and screw down the battery clamp.

The Battery Connexions. Always keep the battery connexions clean, free from corrosion, and tight, otherwise the ammeter readings will *not* indicate the true state of charge of the battery.

THE LIGHTING SET

To prevent trouble the connexions should occasionally be checked for tightness. Also smear them with petroleum jelly.

S.G. Readings (Lucas and Exide Batteries). With Lucas batteries fitted by the makers to all 1945 and later Panthers, the specific gravity readings at an acid temperature of approximately 60°F.* should be: 1·270–1·290, battery fully charged; about 1·190–1·210, battery about half discharged; 1·110–1·150, battery fully discharged.

With Exide batteries fitted by the makers to 1938–40 Panthers with Miller lighting equipment, the specific gravity readings at an acid temperature of approximately 60°F. should be: 1·250, battery fully charged; 1·180, battery about half discharged; 1·110, battery fully discharged. The specific gravity of the acid in the cells when the battery is fully charged should be within 0·005 above or 0·010 below the Exide figure quoted.

Note that specific gravity readings are affected by the temperature of the electrolyte when the readings are taken. Where the temperature of the electrolyte is not 60°F., the specific gravity readings indicated by the hydrometer will not convey the exact state of charge of the battery until the necessary temperature correction has been made, but for 10°F. the variations are not big.

Always check specific gravity readings *after* a run on charge has been made in a case where the battery has just been topped-up. S.G. readings are not reliable until the acid and distilled water have been thoroughly mixed by the gassing of the cells which occurs during charging.

Never permit the battery to remain in a discharged condition for any length of time, or the plates will become badly sulphated. Sometimes a low state of charge is caused by parking the machine for long periods with the lighting switch in the *L* position, without doing much daylight riding. The remedy, of course, is to keep the switch in the *off* position as much as possible and undertake the maximum amount of daylight running with the switch in this position. Should the dynamo persistently overcharge the battery, get an expert to check over the setting of the compensated-voltage-control unit.

When Battery is Out of Use. The battery must *never* be permitted to stand for any lengthy period without being charged. Do not remove the electrolyte and allow the plates to dry, or serious loss of capacity will ensue and the battery may be ruined. It must be removed and periodically charged from some independent source of electrical energy during any period when you cannot charge it on your Panther.

* 60°F. is equivalent to 16°C.

It is best to entrust battery charging to a professional expert who undertakes charging as part of his normal business.

CARE OF LAMPS

This section tells you how to obtain maximum road illumination, assuming that you keep the dynamo and battery effectively operational as already described.

Miller and Lucas Lighting Switch Positions. Compensated voltage control is provided on all 1939 and later Panthers, and therefore the dynamo charges the battery when the engine is running with the lighting switch in any of its three positions which are as follows—

Off: Headlamp, rear lamp, speedometer, and sidecar lamp (when fitted) switched off.

L: Headlamp pilot bulb, rear lamp, speedometer, and sidecar lamp (where fitted) on.

H: Headlamp main bulb, rear lamp, speedometer, and sidecar lamp (where fitted) on.

On 1938 models the headlamp switch has a *CH* (charge) position, the other positions being as above (no charging in *Off* and *L* positions).

For advice on charging (pre-1939) see page 61.

Adjusting Headlamp Position. If the headlamp is incorrectly aligned and/or the main bulb is out of focus, maximum road illumination will not be obtainable, and other road users may be inconvenienced by dazzle. It is easy to rectify both faults.

The best method of checking the alignment of the headlamp is to stand your Panther facing a light-coloured wall at a distance of approximately 25 ft. Switch on the main driving light and note if the beam is projected straight ahead and parallel with the ground.

Take vertical measurements from the centre of the headlamp, and from the centre of the illuminated circle on the wall, to the ground. Both measurements should be equal. If they are unequal, loosen the two fixing bolts securing the headlamp in the front-fork mounting brackets and tilt the headlamp as required. Afterwards tighten the two fixing bolts firmly. Alternatively have the headlamp alignment tested on a Lucas Beamsetter provided at most garages.

Correct Focusing. On all new Panthers the double-filament main bulb is carefully focused to give the best illumination. Provided that Lucas or Miller bulbs of the correct wattage and number are fitted as replacements, subsequent refocusing should not be necessary, unless the focusing adjustment has been disturbed. Late 1951 and subsequent models with the Lucas SSU700P, SSU700P/1, MCH58 or MCH61 headlamp have a main bulb which is permanently "pre-focused."

Widely converging and diverging beams are highly undesirable as they illuminate the road poorly and are liable to dazzle other

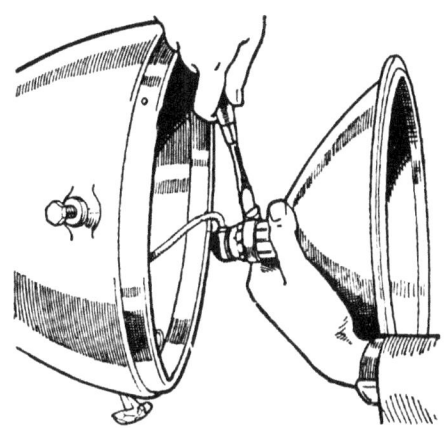

FIG. 32. SLACKENING BULB HOLDER FOR FOCUSING
(1945-50 LUCAS HEADLAMPS)

road users. Adjust the focus of the headlamp immediately if its *beam* is not uniform, is too wide, is of short range, or has a dark centre. To focus the headlamp (not possible on late 1951 and subsequent models) it is necessary to move the main bulb holder backwards or forwards on the reflector axis until the beam is properly focused.

To Focus Lucas DU42 Headlamp (1945-7). Take your Panther to a level stretch of road and focus the headlamp against a light-coloured wall about 25 ft. away. First remove the lamp front and reflector; afterwards release the spring fixing clip which secures the base of the lamp front and pull the latter outwards. As the lamp front and the reflector come away together, free the top tag of the lamp front from the lamp body by lifting the front slightly upwards.

The double-filament main bulb holder is adjustable in the plate fitted to the back of the reflector and, as may be seen in Fig. 32, there is a clamping clip for focusing adjustment. To focus the bulb, loosen the clamping screw on the clip (Fig. 32) and push the bulb holder in or out of the clamping clip as required. Several focusing adjustments may be needed. After each adjustment, replace the lamp front and reflector and test the beam for focus against the wall. When the correct focus is obtained, tighten the screw on the bulb-holder clamping clip firmly.

When fitting the lamp front and reflector, first locate the top tag in the slot of the lamp body. Finally fasten the lamp front by means of the front fixing clip at the base of the lamp.

How to Remove Reflector (Lucas DU42 Headlamp). Remove the four spring clips which secure the reflector and glass to the headlamp front and detach the reflector, the cork packing strip between the reflector and glass, and the glass itself.

To assemble the reflector and glass, use the following procedure. First position the glass in the lamp front. Next fit the cork packing strip to the reflector edge by pressing it into the pins which are integral with the lamp front. Then replace the reflector assembly (complete with bulb holders) on top of the glass. See that the top of the reflector registers with the top of the lamp front. Finally replace and space uniformly the four spring clips.

To Focus Lucas MU42 Headlamp (1948-9). Take your Panther to a level stretch of road and proceed to focus the MU42 headlamp against a light-coloured wall about 25 ft. away. If a focusing adjustment is necessary, first remove the lamp front and reflector.

To remove them, release the spring catch at the bottom of the lamp. The reflector is secured to the body of the MU42 headlamp by means of a rubber bead, and can be withdrawn after its removal.

To focus the lamp after removing the front and reflector, slacken the clamping clip at the back of the reflector (see Fig. 32) and move the bulb holder backwards or forwards as required.

When replacing the rubber bead, locate the thinner lip of the bead between the rim of the reflector and the edge of the lamp body. To replace the lamp front, locate the metal tongue in the slot at the top of the lamp, press the front on, and secure by means of the fixing catch.

To Focus SSU700P Headlamp (1950-1). If a pre-focused bulb is not fitted, focusing should be effected on a level stretch of road with the headlamp beam directed against a wall some 25 ft. distant. Note the general remarks on pages 66-7 concerning correct focusing and alignment.

To remove the front rim, complete with the Lucas light-unit assembly, loosen the securing screw on top of the headlamp body and then withdraw the rim outward from the top, and as the lamp front emerges, raise it a little to free the lower metal

THE LIGHTING SET

tongue from the headlamp shell. The twin-filament (1950) bulb holder is adjustable and has a clamp tightened by one screw.

To focus the main bulb (1950 lamps without "pre-focus" bulb) loosen this screw (see Fig. 32) and push the bulb holder inwards or outwards until the correct focus is obtained. Afterwards firmly tighten the screw which clamps the bulb holder. Next engage the lower metal tongue on the lamp rim with the small slot in the lamp shell, and carefully force the top of the rim back over the lamp shell. Finally retighten the securing screw on the top of the lamp body. On machines later than August, 1950, there is no focusing adjustment (see Fig. 33).

Removing Lucas Light-unit (SSU700P Headlamp).
To remove the reflector and glass assembly from the lamp rim, detach the five spring clips which are spaced evenly round the rim, and withdraw the assembly. When replacing the reflector and glass, lay the assembly on the rim, being careful to engage the block on the reflector back with the forked bracket on the rim. Then replace the five spring-clips which secure the assembly. Note that the glass and reflector are not detachable.

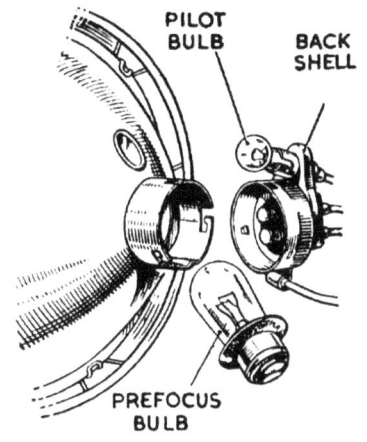

FIG. 33. LUCAS LIGHT-UNIT ASSEMBLY AND "PRE-FOCUSED" MAIN BULB (1950 ONWARDS)

Applies from August, 1950, to late 1951. Late 1951-4 SSU700P/1 lamps have an underslung pilot lamp. On 1955-66 Lucas headlamps the pilot-bulb holder is a push-in fit in the reflector.

The Lucas SSU700P/1 Headlamp (1951-4).
This headlamp (fitted to late 1951 and 1952-4 Panthers) is similar to the SSU700P lamp already dealt with, but a "pre-focused" Lucas bulb (see Fig. 33) is used as on late 1950-1 SSU700P headlamps, and the pilot bulb shows through a separate glass beneath the main glass. The "pre-focused" bulb may be fitted either way round, and no focusing is required. Instructions for removing and fitting the lamp front and light-unit assembly are the same as for the SSU700P headlamp.

The Lucas MCH55, MCH58, MCH61 Headlamps (1955 Onwards).
An attractive feature is the neat installation of the built-in lighting switch, ammeter, and speedometer. These three headlamps have a double-filament "pre-focus" main bulb, requiring no focusing; the pilot bulb is positioned below the main bulb and

its holder is a push-in fit in the reflector of the Lucas light-unit assembly comprising the "sealed beam" glass and reflector unit.

To obtain access to the main and pilot bulbs, loosen the small securing screw on top of the headlamp body and withdraw the rim (complete with light-unit assembly) outward from the top, and as the lamp front emerges, raise it a little to release the lower metal tongue from the lamp shell. The fitting of replacement bulbs is dealt with under this heading on page 72. To replace the light-unit assembly, complete with front rim, engage the lower

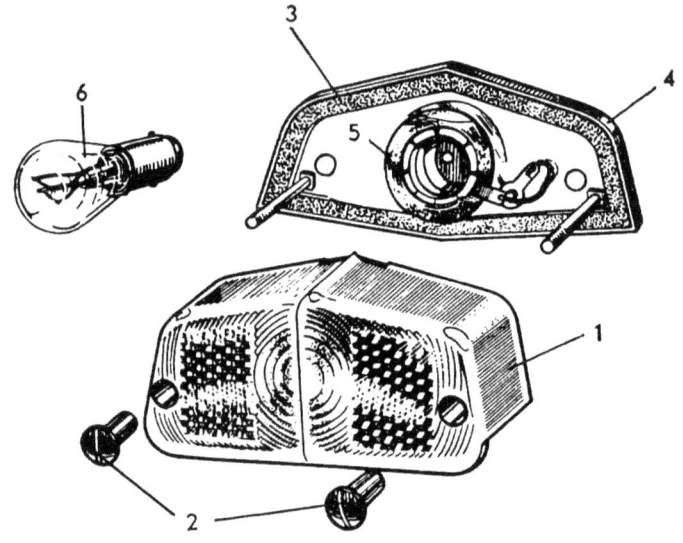

Fig. 34. The Lucas 564 Stop-tail Lamp (1954 Onwards)
1. Red plastic cover with reflex reflector.
2. Slotted nuts.
3. Gasket.
4. Body of lamp.
5. Grummet.
6. Double-filament bulb.

metal tongue on the lamp rim with the small slot in the lamp shell, and gently force the top of the rim back over the lamp shell. Afterwards firmly retighten the securing screw on the top of the lamp body.

To Focus Miller 84E Headlamp (1938-40). With the machine facing a light-coloured wall and about 25 ft. away from it, make a focusing adjustment until a small diameter, uniform beam without a black centre is obtained. If headlamp alignment is not correct attend to this also (see page 66).

To make a focusing adjustment, remove the lamp front, but not the reflector. After inserting a Miller bulb until the bayonet fixing pins have arrived home, a further twisting force to the right enables the bulb and holder to slide either backwards or forwards, and on removing the extra twisting force the bulb is locked in position. The range of backward or forward movement is sufficient to meet all normal requirements.

The Lucas 564 Stop-tail Lamp (1954 Onwards). This stop-tail lamp combines a reflector with the red plastic cover and takes a double-filament 6-volt, 6/18-watt No. 383 or 384 Lucas bulb with bayonet fixing. To obtain access to the bulb, remove the two securing screws and withdraw the plastic cover (see Fig. 34).

Bulb Renewal. If a bulb fails, renew it with a bulb of the correct type. Most large accessory dealers and garages stock Lucas and Miller bulbs, which are all carefully tested by the makers to ensure that the filament is correctly positioned to give maximum lighting.

Do not wait until actual burning-out occurs, but renew bulbs when they have been in prolonged service. You will thus avoid the risk of incorrect focusing caused by sagging filaments.

Never buy cheap and inferior bulbs which often have their filaments shaped so that correct focusing is not obtainable. Lucas bulbs have their metal caps marked with a number for identification, and when renewing a bulb make sure that the number on the cap (e.g. 168 or 312) is identical to the number on the cap of the original bulb.

Lucas Bulb Replacements (1945 Onwards). Fit in the Lucas DU42 and MU42 headlamps (1945-9) a Lucas No. 168 6-volt, 24-watt, double-filament main bulb. The correct pilot bulb is a Lucas No. 200, 6-volt, 3-watt type.

On a 1950 Lucas SSU700P headlamp (without "pre-focused" main bulb) fit a Lucas No. 169, 6-volt, 30-watt, double-filament main bulb, and a Lucas No. 988 6-volt, 3-watt pilot bulb.

On the 1950 Lucas SSU700P headlamp (with "pre-focused" main bulb) and on the Lucas SSU700P/1 headlamp (late 1951 to 1954), the correct "pre-focused" main bulb is a Lucas No. 312, 6-volt, 30/24-watt type, and the correct pilot bulb is a Lucas No. 988 6-volt, 3-watt bulb. The same type "pre-focus" main bulb (No. 312) is also suitable for the 1955-66 Lucas MCH55, MCH58 and MCH61 headlamps, and note that the correct pilot bulb for the lamps is a Lucas No. 951 M.C.C., 6-volt, 6-watt bulb.

Note that Lucas double-filament "pre-focused" bulbs have a broad locating flange on the cap (instead of a bayonet fixing) and cannot be fitted to headlamps of the focusing type.

For a Model 100 or 120 sidecar lamp if you own a sidecar

outfit, use a pilot bulb; i.e No. 200 or No. 988. But first check the sidecar lamp to make sure which pilot bulb will fit; for 1945-53 Lucas rear lamps fit a 6-volt, 6-watt No. 205 bulb.

Where a Lucas 564 stop-tail lamp is fitted (1954 onwards) the correct double-filament bulb to fit is a Lucas No. 384, 6-volt, 6/18-watt double-filament bulb.

Miller Bulb Replacements (1938-40). The Miller headlamp, type 84E, used in conjunction with the 6-volt, 36-watt Miller DM3G dynamo (1938 models) and also the 6-volt, 36-watt dynamo on the Miller "Dyno-mag" (1939-40 models) requires a Miller 6-volt, 24-watt, double-filament main bulb, and a Miller 6-volt, 3-watt pilot bulb. A 6-volt, 6-watt bulb is also suitable for the Miller, type 36E, rear lamp; fit a 6-volt, 3-watt bulb in the sidecar lamp (where fitted).

Fitting Replacement Bulbs. Where a Lucas DU42 headlamp (1945-7) or a Lucas MU headlamp (1948-9) is concerned, the main and pilot bulbs are accessible for renewal when the front rim and glass assembly are removed as described on page 68.

With a Lucas SSU700P focusing headlamp (1950), to obtain access to the bulbs for renewal, remove the front rim and light unit assembly (see page 68). Then to remove the cap which carries the two bulb holders, depress one of the two spring-loaded plungers securing the cap to the reflector and tilt the cap bodily. When replacing the main-bulb holder, engage the bulb-holder carrier cap in the position where the pilot bulb is against the small window in the reflector (see Fig. 33).

To renew a "pre-focused" main bulb (August, 1950 onwards), turn the back shell (see Fig. 33) anti-clockwise, pull off, and remove the bulb. Fit the correct renewal bulb in the holder, engage the two projections on the inside of the back shell with the slots in the bulb holder, press on, and secure by turning clockwise.

To remove the pilot bulb from a Lucas SSU700P/1 headlamp (1951-4), remove the lamp front and pull out the metal carrier-plate which holds the bulb. On 1955-7 Lucas MCH55, MCH58 and MCH61 headlamps it is only necessary to remove the lamp front and pull out the pilot-bulb holder from the rear of the reflector.

With the Miller headlamp, type 84E, remove the lamp front and glass to obtain access to the bulbs.

A bayonet-type fixing for attaching bulbs to bulb holders is provided for all Lucas (except "pre-focus") and Miller lamps (headlamp, rear lamp, and sidecar lamp, where included). To remove a bulb from its holder, release the bayonet fixing and withdraw the bulb.

THE LIGHTING SET

When renewing a double-filament main bulb (except "prefocus") the new bulb must be fitted the correct way round, i.e. with the *dipped-beam filament above the centre filament*. On Lucas main bulbs the word "Top" is usually etched to indicate the correct position of the bulb in its holder. If the position of a bulb holder has been disturbed when renewing a bulb, check the focus of the headlamp (see page 66). Where a bulb holder has not been disturbed and a Lucas or Miller replacement bulb is fitted, refocusing should not normally be necessary. If in any doubt, check the focus.

Cleaning Lucas and Miller Lamps. The reflector is most important. Never scratch its surface during handling, and avoid finger-marking the surface, readily done on Lucas DU42 and MU42 headlamps (not of the "sealed beam" type).

Never clean the reflector with metal polish. Lucas reflectors have a colourless and transparent protective covering. To clean any finger marks from this covering, polish the surface gently with a chamois leather or with a clean, *very soft* dry cloth such as a "Selvyt." Its use, in conjunction with a little jeweller's rouge, is recommended by H. Miller & Co., Ltd.

Clean the black surfaces of the lamp body with a good car polish, and polish the chromium-plated rim with a chamois leather or a soft, dry cloth, after first washing off any dirt with some water.

THE ELECTRIC HORN

No adjustment to a Clear Hooters (1938-40) or Lucas horn (1945 onwards) is normally desirable until a very big mileage has been covered. A minor adjustment to improve horn performance may then give satisfactory results. If it does not, do not dismantle the horn but return it to a Lucas service depot for expert attention. Note that an uncertain horn action resulting in a choking sound or complete failure of the diaphragm to vibrate does not necessarily imply a horn fault. Possible causes of the trouble are: a loose fixing bolt; vibration of some adjacent point; a discharged battery; a loose connexion; a short circuit in the wiring; or a defective horn push switch.

To Adjust Lucas Type HF1234 Horn. The Lucas type HF1234 horn is provided on most 1945-63 Model 100 and 120 Panthers. Except on a few 1950-1 horns a small adjusting screw is fitted at the back of the horn. To make an adjustment to offset loss of power and roughness, depress the horn push and turn the adjusting screw *anti-clockwise* until the horn ceases to sound. Then release the horn push and turn the adjusting screw *clockwise* six notches, equivalent to one-quarter of a turn. Should further adjustment be necessary, turn the adjusting screw clockwise one notch at a time.

To Adjust Lucas Type 6H Horn. The Lucas type 6H horn is fitted to 1964-6 Model 120 Panthers. To take up wear in the moving parts and reduce roughness and lack of performance, operate the horn push and slowly turn the adjustment screw (located at the back of the horn) *anti-clockwise* until the horn just ceases to sound. Then release the horn push and turn the adjustment screw *clockwise* one notch at a time until the original performance of the horn is restored. Usually it is necessary to turn the adjustment screw one-quarter to three-quarters of a turn. Do not attempt to dismantle the horn, and on no account disturb the slotted centre screw and lock-nut. This applies to both types of Lucas horns.

THE WIRING CIRCUIT

The wiring circuit, with cables braided to form a neat harness, is simple and readily comprehended by reference to the wiring diagrams on pages 75-8. If the wires (identified by coloured sleevings) are correctly connected and the connexions are kept firm and clean, there is no risk of an excessive surge of current damaging the wiring circuit. Hence *no fuse* whatever is incorporated.

Examine the Wiring Occasionally. It is advisable periodically carefully to examine the wiring. Before making any alterations or removing the lighting switch, first disconnect the positive or negative lead from the battery (see page 58).

See that all connexions are tight and clean, and that the insulation at all points is sound. Pay special attention to the positive lead from the dynamo to the lighting switch (via the C.V.C. unit) and the lead from the battery to the "B" terminal of the ammeter (or switch). Faulty dynamo leads may suddenly cause the dynamo to stop charging.

Dynamo Leads to C.V.C. Unit. Never reverse the leads connected to the *D* and *F* terminals of the Lucas dynamo and regulator unit (see Fig. 29). To prevent this, the screw in the dynamo terminal block is off-centre and the screws securing the regulator clamping plate are of different size.

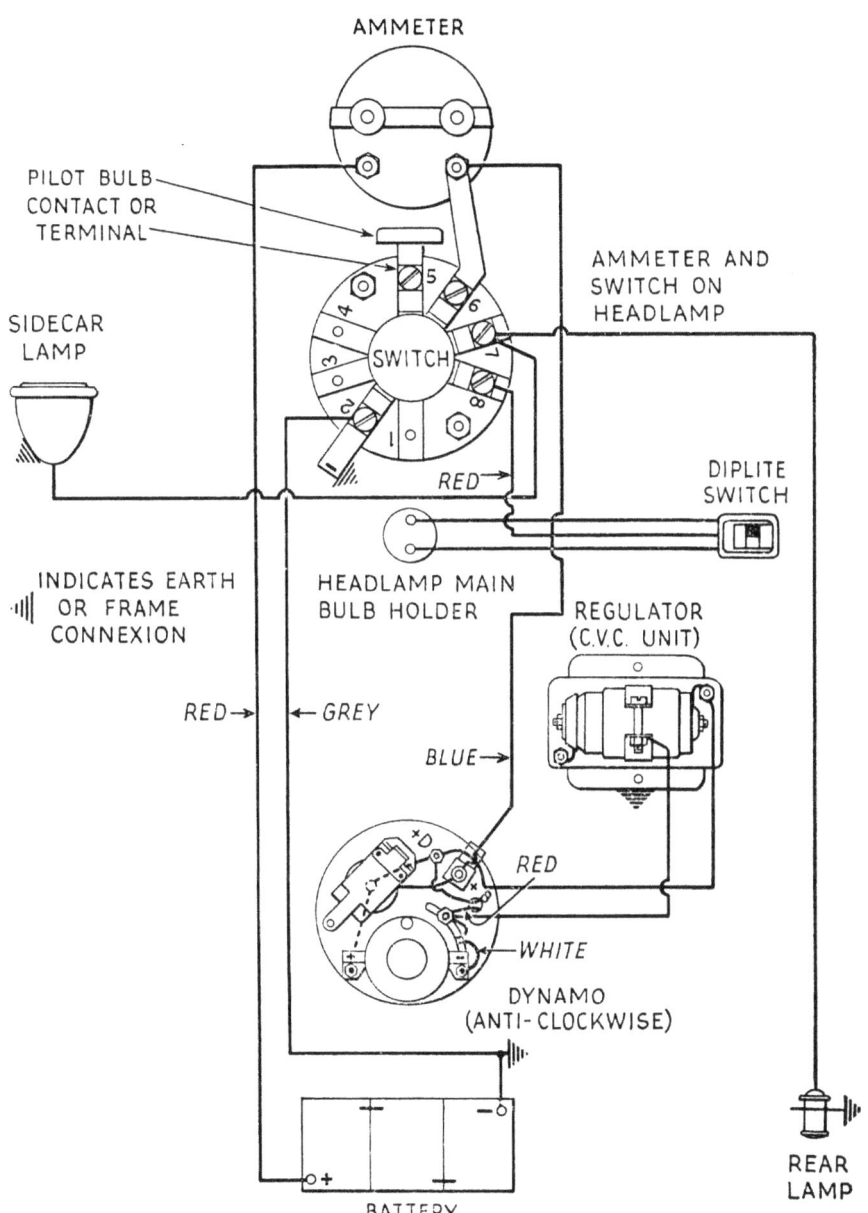

Fig. 35. Wiring Diagram for 1939-40 Model 100 Panthers
(*H. Miller & Co., Ltd.*)

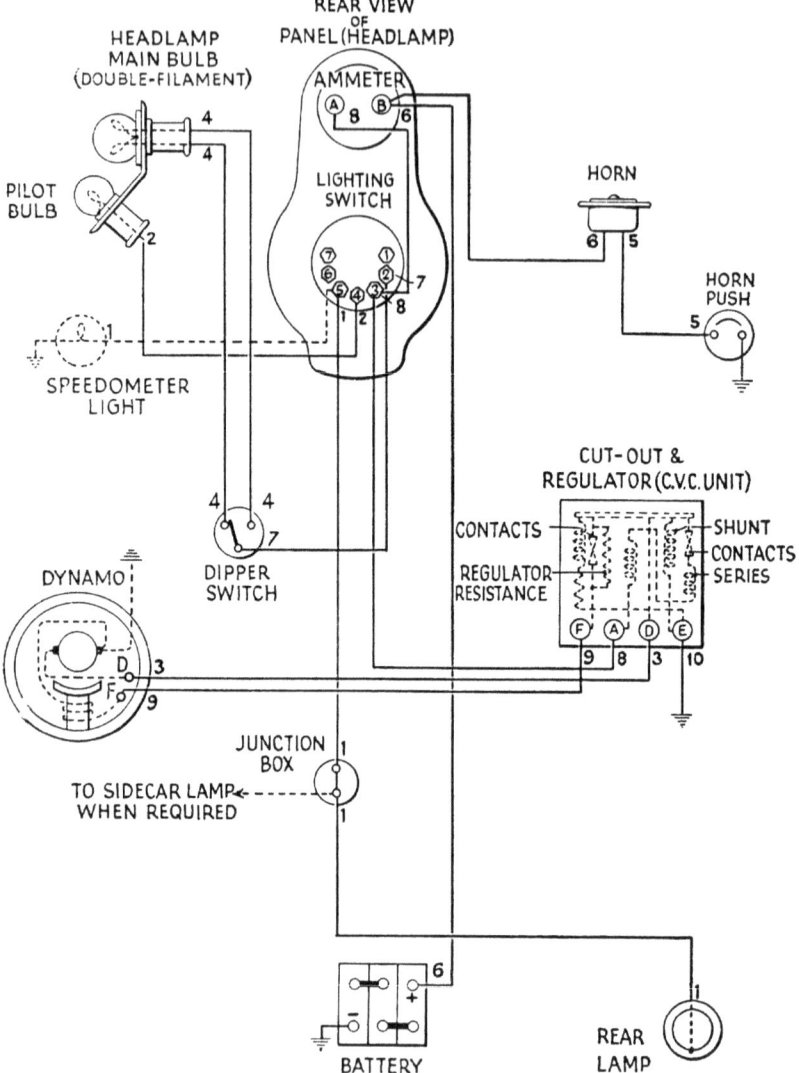

Fig. 36. Wiring Diagram (Negative Earth) for 1945–51 Model 100 Panthers

(*Joseph Lucas, Ltd.*)

The numbers indicate the colours of the wiring sleeves.

Key to Sleeving Colours

1. Red.
2. Red and black.
3. Yellow.
4. Blue.
5. Yellow and purple.
6. Yellow and black.
7. Blue and white.
8. White and purple.
9. Green and black.
10. Black.

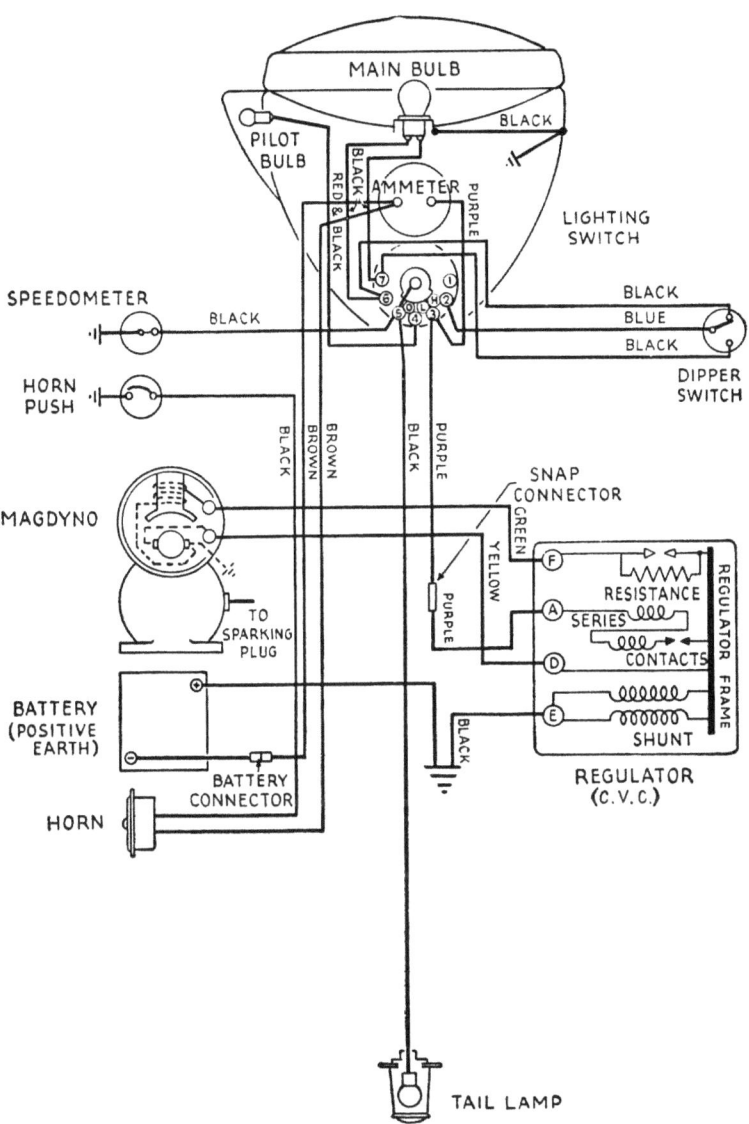

FIG. 37. WIRING DIAGRAM (POSITIVE EARTH) FOR 1952-4 MODEL 100 PANTHERS

(*Joseph Lucas, Ltd.*)

The sleeving colours are shown in the diagram. On the 1955-66 models the pilot bulb is internally located (at the rear of the reflector) and a double-filament stop-tail lamp is provided instead of the tail lamp shown.

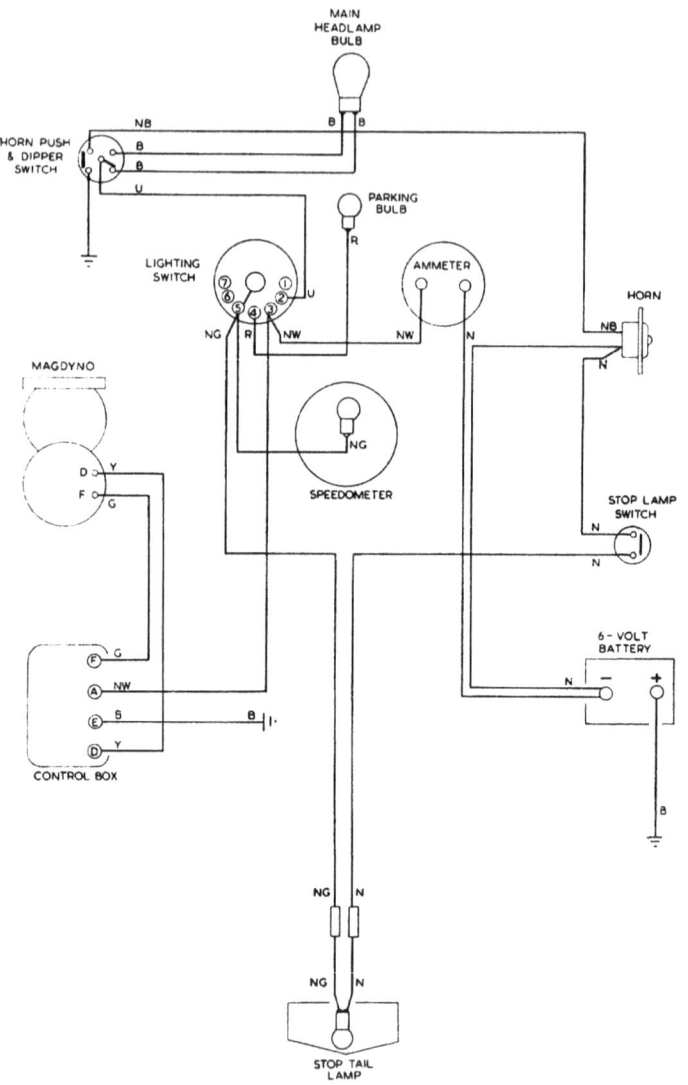

FIG. 38. WIRING DIAGRAM (POSITIVE EARTH) FOR 1955-63 MODEL 100 AND 1959-66 MODEL 120 PANTHERS
(*Joseph Lucas, Ltd.*)

KEY TO SLEEVING COLOURS

B. Black.
G. Green.
N. Brown.

R. Red.
U. Blue.
W. White.
Y. Yellow.

CHAPTER VI

GENERAL MAINTENANCE

FULL maintenance instructions for 1938 and later Models 100 and 120 are given in this chapter. Some of the preceding chapters, however, deal with certain maintenance matters. Appropriate cross-references are therefore included.

Spares and Repairs. Whenever you deliver or forward parts to the makers or to an authorized dealer, attach to each part a label bearing clearly your *full name and address*.

In connexion with spares and repairs, it is worth noting that George Clarke (Motors) Ltd. of 73 New Park Road, London, S.W.2. (Phone: Tulse Hill 3211) have the most comprehensive spare parts stock in the U.K. This firm has a replacement service and also a large selection of used spares at bargain prices. Spares can be obtained c.o.d. by return. Repairs and major overhauls are dealt with by Panther repair specialists.

Another firm specializing in Panther spares is Newton Motors of 397 Manchester Road, Bradford (Phone: Bradford 29719).

Seven Large Accessory Firms. Seven large firms which can meet various requirements are: E. S. Motors, Marble Arch Motor Supplies, Ltd.; The Halford Cycle Co., Ltd.; Turner's Stores; James Grose, Ltd.; George Grose, Ltd.; Claude Rye, Ltd.; Whitbys of Acton, Ltd.; and Pride & Clarke, Ltd.

Items Required for Engine Maintenance. Certain items you *must* have handy in the lock-up or garage. These include: a can of paraffin for cleaning purposes; a stiff brush for scouring dirt off the crankcase; a tin of suitable engine oil (see page 32); a canister of grease; a small oil-can containing some engine oil; a receptacle for oil when draining the oil sump; some dishes or jars for washing engine parts in; some non-fluffy rags; valve grinding paste such as Richford's (coarse and fine): some fine emery cloth; a set of engine gaskets; a pair of gudgeon-pin circlips; some jointing compound; and some good hand cleanser.

The tool kit supplied (shown in Fig. 39) plus a few extras, are sufficient for all normal stripping down and assembly.

It will be observed that a pair of small round-nosed pliers for gudgeon-pin circlip removal is *not* included in the Panther tool kit, and it is desirable to purchase a pair of suitable pliers. It is also necessary to obtain a plug regapping tool with feeler gauges for the sparking plug (see page 46), and a wire brush.

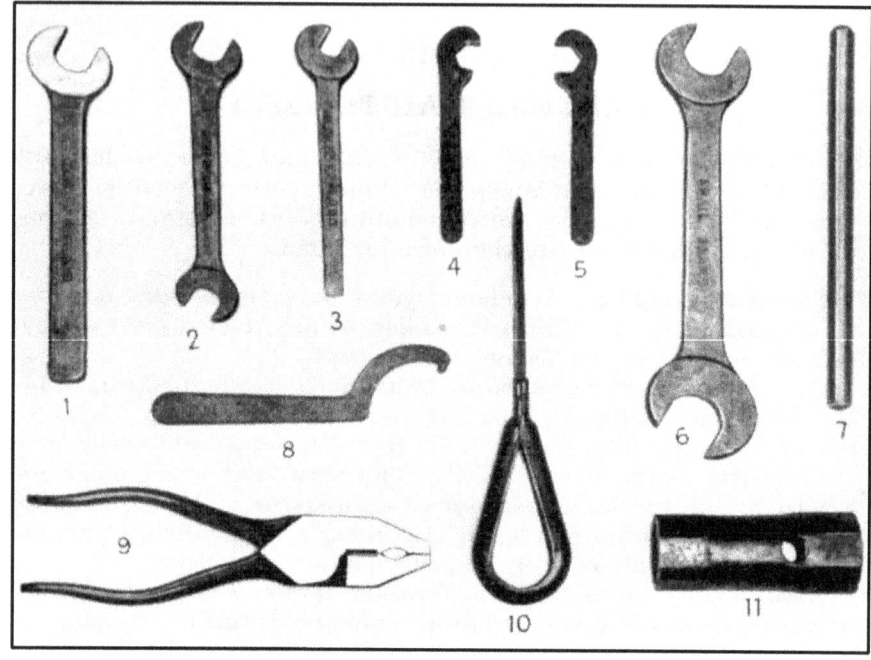

FIG. 39. THE MODEL 100 AND 120 PANTHER TOOL KIT
(1947 ONWARDS)

The earlier tool kit is similar, but different spanners are provided for the girder-type front forks.

1. Single-ended $\frac{5}{16}$ in. Whit. ($\frac{3}{8}$ in. B.S.F.) spanner for petrol-pipe unions and various frame and cylinder head nuts.

2. Double-ended $\frac{1}{4}$ in. × $\frac{5}{16}$ in. Whit. ($\frac{5}{16}$ × $\frac{3}{8}$ in. B.S.F.) spanner for nuts and bolts on front forks, carburettor, and various points on the frame.

3. Single-ended $\frac{1}{8}$ in. Whit. ($\frac{3}{16}$ in. B.S.F.) spanner for secondary chain oil-adjuster, and carburettor float-chamber lid and throttle-stop (pre-1956).

4. Spanner for adjusting tappets.

5. Spanner for adjusting tappets.

6. Double-ended $\frac{3}{8}$ × $\frac{7}{16}$ in. Whit. ($\frac{7}{16}$ × $\frac{1}{2}$ in. B.S.F.) spanner for large nuts on frame, carburettor jet plug, and gearbox fixing bolts.

7. Tommy-bar for box spanner (11).

8. "C" spanner for lower portion of push-rod cover tube.

9. Pliers (with wire cutter).

10. Metal screwdriver.

11. Double-ended box spanner for sparking plug and gearbox fulcrum, and wheel spindle nuts.

Also included, but not illustrated, are a magneto spanner with feeler gauge for contact-breaker, tyre levers, a grease gun (see Fig. 17), and for 1956-66 models a spanner for adjusting the rear-suspension shock-absorber units.

GENERAL MAINTENANCE

To enable you to strip down your engine for decarbonizing and valve grinding you will need also the three tools (obtainable from George Clarke (Motors) Ltd.) illustrated in Fig. 40.

It is also desirable to obtain a suitable gudgeon-pin extractor and frame lug alignment rod (see page 102). If you decide to undertake as much repair work as possible besides routine maintenance, stripping-down, and assembly, it is desirable to rig up a

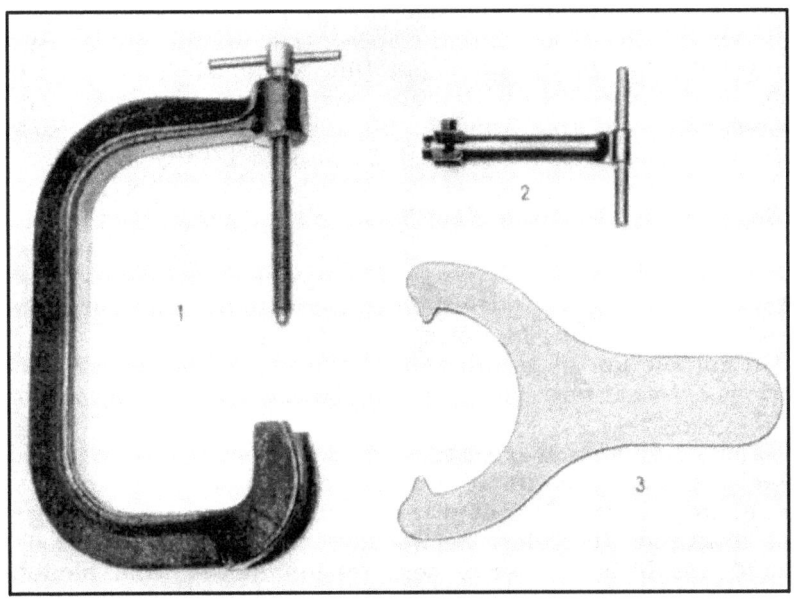

FIG. 40. THREE TOOLS YOU WILL NEED
1. Valve-spring compressor.
3. "C" spanner for exhaust ring-nuts.
2. Valve holder for grinding-in valves (a suction-type holder is now recommended for Panther engines).

suitable bench, complete with vice, and to purchase some extra tools. Repair work is beyond the scope of this handbook, and you need fair technical knowledge and skill in handling tools.

ENGINE MAINTENANCE

Engine lubrication is dealt with fully in Chapter III. Keep the oil sump well topped up.

Carburettor Tuning and Maintenance. For full instructions refer to Chapter II and page 111.

Care of the Ignition System. Comprehensive advice is given in Chapter IV.

Always Keep Engine Thoroughly Clean. Internal and external cleanliness of the engine are essential to its efficiency, quite apart from pride of ownership. Dirt hides defects, may get inside the engine when it is being dismantled, and encourages rusting.

Cylinder and cylinder-head fins should be clean and black. If they become rusted, appearance suffers and there is an appreciable reduction in heat dispersion. Use a stiff brush dipped in paraffin for cleaning the fins. If the enamel has worn away, paint the fins with some cylinder black.

Scour off the filth from the lower part of the crankcase and sump with stiff brushes and paraffin. Clean all aluminium alloy and bright surfaces with rags and paraffin, assisted where necessary by suitable brushes. Thorough cleaning (see also page 115) may take quite a time, but the results are worth while.

See that All Nuts are Kept Tight. Some initial bedding-down of components occurs on a new Panther, and during running-in check over the various nuts and bolts for tightness at frequent intervals. Pay special attention to the cylinder and the cylinder head, and the engine mounting, also the pipe unions.

On completion of running-in it is advisable to check over the various external nuts and bolts for tightness about once a month.

Tappet Adjustment is Important. Incorrect tappet adjustment interferes with the lift of the valves and to some extent the valve timing. Insufficient or no clearances between the tappets and push-rods (therefore between valves and overhead rockers) besides resulting in loss of compression, power, and flexibility, may also distort and/or burn the exhaust valve because of gas leakage.

Excessive valve clearances will not damage the exhaust valve but are likely to cause excessive valve clatter and some loss of efficiency due to reduced valve lift, and late opening of the valves. Always keep the clearances correct. Check them occasionally. Actual tappet adjustment is seldom required unless the engine is new or the valves have recently been ground-in.

To Adjust Tappets (1938 Onwards). Referring to Fig. 41, with the "C" spanner (shown at 8 in Fig. 39), unscrew (anti-clockwise) the threaded portion C of the lower push-rod cover tube G from the threads in the flanged tappet-guide J. On 1957–66 models free the clamp plate. Then push upwards the lower push-rod cover tube so that it telescopes into the upper tube and thereby exposes the push-rods, tappets, and tappet adjusters.

Verify that the decompressor is in the "Off" position (lever up) and that there is some backlash in the exhaust-valve lifter (see

GENERAL MAINTENANCE

page 84). Next remove the sparking plug and turn the engine over slowly by the kick-starter until both valves are fully closed, as indicated by the inlet and exhaust tappets A, K being right down.

When both tappets are right down (at the beginning of the firing stroke) the piston is at approximately top-dead-centre. Now check whether the adjustment of each tappet is correct.

In the case of both inlet and exhaust tappets, the adjustment

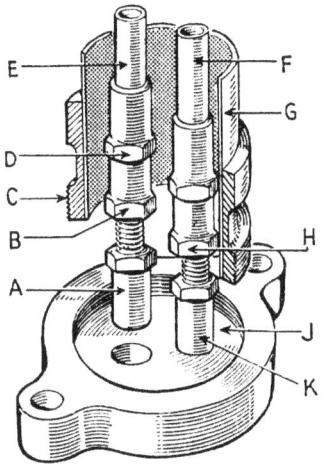

A. Inlet tappet.
B. Lock-nut for inlet-tappet head.
C. Threaded portion of tube G.
D. Hexagon on tappet head (cupped for push-rod).
E. Inlet push-rod.
F. Exhaust push-rod.
G. Push-rod cover tube (lower portion).
H. Lock-nut for exhaust-tappet head.
J. Tappet guide with flange for item C.
K. Exhaust tappet.

FIG. 41. PANTHER TAPPET ADJUSTMENT (1938 ONWARDS)
On all 1957 and later engines tube G is a push fit in the tappet guide and has a clamp plate and oil seals.

should be such that with the *engine warmed up to its normal running temperature* it is possible to rotate the push-rod (E or F) freely with the fingers without any up-and-down movement.

If an inlet or exhaust tappet (the *outer* one) needs adjusting, slacken (clockwise) the lock-nut B or H (Fig. 41) with one of the tappet spanners (shown at 4, 5 in Fig. 39) while holding the tappet head with the other spanner applied to the head hexagon D. Then with one tappet spanner hold the tappet by its hexagon (the bottom one) and with the other spanner applied to the tappet-head hexagon D, screw the tappet head up (anti-clockwise), or down according to whether it is desired to lessen or increase the valve clearance.

When the correct valve clearance is obtained, hold the tappet head with one spanner and with the other retighten the lock-nut B or H securely. Afterwards check the clearances again. Finally, reposition the lower portion of the push-rod cover tube and, with the "C" spanner, screw home its base into the threaded valve-guide flange. On 1957 and later models secure the clamp plate. Also replace the sparking plug and its copper washer.

Backlash in Exhaust-valve Lifter Control. Before checking the valve clearances, and at all other times, allow a little backlash ($\frac{1}{16}-\frac{1}{8}$ in.) at the exhaust-valve lifter on the near side of the handlebars, with the exhaust valve fully closed, otherwise it is impossible for the exhaust valve to seat properly, and loss of compression, power, and burning of the exhaust valve are likely.

An adjustment for the cable stop is provided on top of the rocker-box cover, on the off side (see Fig. 42). Verify that the exhaust valve is *fully* closed. Then to take up cable stretch, pull up the rubber shield, loosen the lock-nut, and turn the adjuster *anti-clockwise* as required. Now retighten the lock-nut.

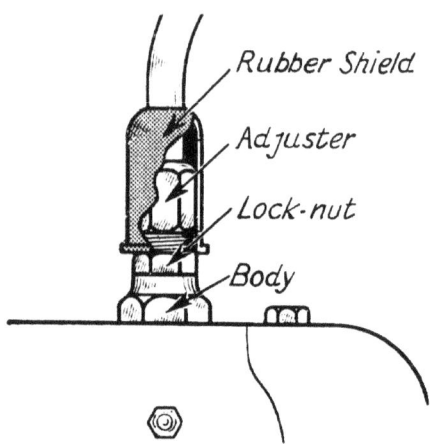

FIG. 42. EXHAUST-VALVE LIFTER ADJUSTMENT
The valve-lifter body is screwed into the rocker cover.

DECARBONIZING AND GRINDING-IN VALVES

Carbon deposits form slowly inside the engine (mainly on the piston crown and inside of the combustion chamber) because of: (*a*) incomplete fuel combustion, (*b*) burning of oil, and (*c*) burning of some road dust.

The formation of carbon inside the engine soon becomes apparent. Gone is that youthful liveliness and power; the motor-cycle begins to shy at gradients up which it normally romps, and emits a metallic knocking sound under slight provocation (generally when the load is suddenly increased). The exhaust becomes "woolly" and the engine tends to overheat.

If these symptoms develop after a considerable mileage, they indicate that decarbonizing is *overdue*. But it is advisable to decarbonize and, if necessary, grind-in the valves whenever needed, and not to wait until the engine becomes really filthy inside. Decarbonizing is really quite simple.

Under normal conditions it is advisable to decarbonize a new (or reconditioned) engine after the first 2,000 miles (approximately) and thereafter to decarbonize it at regular intervals exceeding 3,000 miles. If you ride carefully and always keep your mount in

GENERAL MAINTENANCE

good condition, the mileage between decarbonizing can be increased appreciably (say, up to 5,000 miles).

Getting Ready for the Job. With your Panther jacked up on its rear or centre stand, get out the tool kit (see Fig. 39). Have also available the tools shown in Fig. 40, and a tin of *fine-grade* valve-grinding paste.

If piston removal is contemplated, you will also need a small pair of snipe-nosed pliers and an extractor (see page 91) for gudgeon-pin removal, together with a new pair of gudgeon-pin circlips. For piston ring removal three thin metal strips will be required (see page 94). For the actual job of "decoking" you need a proprietary scraper or a blunt screwdriver. For engine reassembly it is convenient to have a $\frac{1}{2}$ in. diameter frame-lug alignment rod or tube (see page 102).

In addition to the items just mentioned, it is also desirable to have at hand a new cylinder-base washer and also a cylinder-head gasket, in case the old ones are damaged. Finally, you will need a receptacle containing paraffin, a few clean rags, engine oil, and some clean paper on which to lay the various engine parts as they are removed. Some low boxes for storage of engine components are useful.

If the engine is very dirty externally, give it a good clean up (see page 82), to facilitate stripping-down and prevent dirt getting inside. Having got everything ready for decarbonizing, consider what amount of stripping-down is really called for and the decarbonizing procedure to be followed.

General Decarbonizing Procedure. To prevent unnecessary waste of time and labour, and to ensure maximum efficiency, note carefully the following six points—

1. Petrol tank removal *is* essential.

2. Complete removal of the engine from the frame is quite unnecessary on *all* 1938–63 598 c.c. Model 100 engines. It is also not necessary on 645 c.c. Model 120 engines except on 1959–61 types where spanner holds are not provided at the bottom of the four long rods passing right through the engine. In this case decarbonizing *does* necessitate complete removal of the engine from the frame.

3. For a normal strip, remove only the cylinder head and associated parts (dealt with in sections 1–5, pages 86–9), and then scrape off the carbon deposits from the piston crown, the combustion chamber, and the valve ports.

4. Remove the valves from the cylinder head each time the engine is decarbonized so that the ports can be thoroughly cleaned, and grind-in both the valves unless this is genuinely unnecessary.

Never grind-in the valves more than is necessary to ensure a gas-tight seal.

5. Do *not* remove the cylinder barrel unnecessarily, as this disturbs the piston rings which is undesirable more often than is absolutely essential.

6. Withdraw the cylinder barrel and remove the piston only if the piston rings and grooves require inspection and cleaning (advised where bad compression exists in spite of the valves and their seats being in perfect condition, and when oil consumption is high).

The full procedure for decarbonizing and grinding-in the valves of your Panther engine is described in detail in the following sections 1-27, of this chapter.* How much stripping-down is required depends on whether you decide to remove the cylinder barrel and piston in addition to the cylinder head, a point which has already been referred to in the preceding notes 5 and 6.

DECARBONIZING PROCEDURE—598 C.C. MODEL 100 ENGINE (1938-63)

1. Remove the Petrol Tank. The removal of the petrol tank is a necessary preliminary to decarbonizing and indeed to all major stripping-down and overhauling operations.

To remove the petrol tank (1938 onwards), first turn off both petrol taps and disconnect the fuel pipe from both taps and from the carburettor float-chamber. Use two spanners, and when unscrewing each pipe union-nut, hold the tap hexagon with one spanner to avoid straining the joint at the tank.

Sever the wire (where fitted) which locks the front pair of vertical bolts (they have drilled heads) securing the tank to the two horizontal support lugs at the forward end of the frame top-tube. Unscrew these short vertical bolts† and remove each bolt, together with the steel washer and lower rubber pad (see Fig. 43). Each upper rubber pad (provided between the tank support and the tank) can be removed when the tank is subsequently lifted off.

Now remove the long horizontal stud securing the two vertical support lugs (at the rear of the tank) to the frame. Remove the split-pin (or wire) from one end of the stud and also remove one of the two nuts and its washer (slightly smaller than the front pair). Then push or tap out the stud from the side from which the nut is removed.

* Note that where the numbered sub-headings to sections are worded as positive instructions (i.e., sub-headings to sections numbered 1-5, 13, 14, 15, 18, and 23 onwards) the operations described *must* be attended to *every time* the engine is decarbonized. See also page 104.

† It is good practice first to loosen the two vertical front securing bolts and the rear horizontal stud before removing them individually.

GENERAL MAINTENANCE

Lift off the tank upwards and to the rear. Do not smoke when doing this. Be careful not to lose the two rubber pads on top of the front support lugs and the two rubber pads at the rear, one on the *inside* of each vertical support-lug brazed to the rear of the tank.

After removing the petrol tank, place it in a safe position. Also keep together (and remember their positions) the two short bolts, the long stud, the six rubber pads, and the four steel washers.

2. Remove the Exhaust Pipe(s) and Silencer(s). Before attempting to remove the cylinder head "clear the deck" as much as

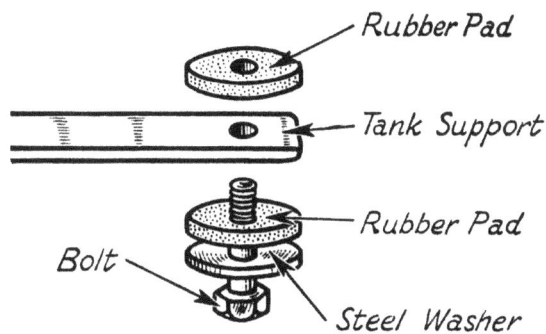

FIG. 43. OFF-SIDE SUPPORT FOR FRONT OF PETROL TANK
The near-side support is identical. A single horizontal double-ended stud is used for the rear tank support

possible. With the "C" spanner (3, Fig. 40) unscrew the finned ring-nut(s) securing the exhaust pipe(s) to the cylinder-head port(s). Do not use a drift.

Loosen the bolt(s) connecting the Panther silencer(s) to the rear of the frame and then draw the exhaust pipe(s) clear of the cylinder head. On 1957-66 models remove the bracket nuts. You can then remove completely the exhaust pipe(s) with silencer(s) attached. This will allow the exhaust system to be cleaned thoroughly. Do not scratch the chromium plating.

3. Prepare to Remove Cylinder Head. Begin the engine strip as follows: Remove the air filter (if used), and carburettor from the induction pipe after unscrewing its two securing bolts. See that the washer between the induction pipe and carburettor flanges is not damaged. To disconnect the carburettor controls (see Fig. 52), unscrew the mixing-chamber cap 2 (knurled) and withdraw from the mixing chamber the mixing-chamber top 28, together with the air and throttle valves 3, 26.

Place the carburettor in a box or on a clean piece of paper. It is most important that no dirt is permitted to enter the carburettor. Before laying the carburettor aside, check that its induction flange face is not distorted through excessive tightening of the attachment bolts. If a straightedge reveals appreciable distortion (concave face), grind the face of the flange dead true.

Next remove the sparking plug and its copper washer; also disconnect the external delivery and return oil-pipes connected between the crankcase and cylinder head fore and aft of the cylinder. The pipe union-nuts can readily be removed with the appropriate spanner in the tool kit.

With the "C" spanner (8, Fig. 39) unscrew the base of the lower push-rod cover tube and telescope this portion into the upper portion. Also remove the two screws which secure the flange of the upper portion to the cylinder head. A thin paper washer is provided at this joint.

Raise the exhaust-valve lifter, and rotate the engine with the kick-starter until all pressure on the control is released, and then disconnect the exhaust-valve lifter control cable at the lever. The exhaust-valve lifter can be left connected at the rocker cover. Afterwards rotate the engine until the inlet and exhaust valves are fully closed.

4. Remove the Cylinder Head. After removing the petrol tank and other parts as described in sections 1–3, remove the cylinder head itself. The procedure on all 1938 and later engines is as follows.

First remove the bolt securing the top engine-mounting lugs to the frame, and knock out the two steel bushes or cups and rubber bushes. Next remove the top engine-mounting lugs from the cylinder head. To do this, remove the four securing screws. The lug supports on the off side pass through the rocker cover, but no oil seals are necessary or provided.

Remove evenly, and diagonally, the seven screws securing the rocker cover to the cylinder head. Note that the *centre* securing screw on the off side is *longer* than the remaining six screws. Place this longer screw aside separately to ensure its correct replacement, otherwise the cylinder head may be damaged.

Now rotate the engine with the kick-starter until the exhaust valve opens; it is still impossible to lift off the rocker cover, because the exhaust valve-lifter lever fouls it. Remove the valve-lifter lever from its fulcrum by pulling the lever *towards* you. Now lift away the rocker cover. You can then take off the two push-rods and the overhead rockers, although, if preferred, you can remove them as the cylinder head is taken off. Mark the push-rods to ensure their being replaced in the same positions.

GENERAL MAINTENANCE

Remove the four nuts from the upper ends of the two "U" rods which run for the full length of the engine, and also *slacken* the two additional nuts provided (on inverted studs) between the cylinder-head fins, fore and aft, to secure the head to the cylinder barrel. Push the engine rods down, or tap them down very gently, until they are just clear of the cylinder-head face.*

Lift off the cylinder head from the cylinder barrel. As you raise the head slightly, *remove* the two fore and aft nuts from the inverted cylinder-head studs. These nuts cannot be removed from between the fins until the head is lifted slightly. If the joint is stiff, tap lightly beneath one of the exhaust ports with a suitable piece of hardwood. Do not attempt to prise off the cylinder head with a screwdriver or other implement, otherwise you may damage the copper gasket between the head and barrel faces. This gasket must be perfect. Remove the gasket, or scrap it if there are any signs of damage or of "blowing." If the gasket has become "hard," anneal it by heating it until it discolours and then plunging it into cold water. Cover the top of the cylinder barrel with a cloth.

5. Remove the Valves. The inlet and exhaust valves should be removed about every 3,000-5,000 miles when the engine is stripped for decarbonizing. Remove the valves after taking off the cylinder head and *before* any attempt is made to clean the valve ports. It is convenient to remove the valves in comfort on a bench.

The best method of removing the valves is to use the Panther valve-spring compressor (1, Fig. 40). It is assumed that the inlet and exhaust overhead rockers have been removed clear of the valve stems. Remove each of the two valves; position the valve-spring compressor so that its slotted end fits over the valve-spring upper collar (see Fig. 47) and the pointed end of the screw contacts the centre of the valve head.

With the tommy-bar tighten the compressor screw until the duplex valve-spring is compressed enough to permit the removal of the split collet (holding the upper collar to the valve stem). If the split collet (a taper fit in the collar) is stiff, tap it sharply, but be careful not to lose the collet halves as they come off the valve stem. You can now withdraw the valve and remove the inner and outer valve springs, with the upper and lower collars.

After removing both valves, springs, etc., lay the parts on a clean sheet of paper and be most careful not to interchange the inlet and exhaust valves which are ground on to their seats individually. They must *always* be kept on their original seats

---

* To permit the near-side engine rod (see Fig. 53) to be pushed down, you may have to unscrew the bolt securing the primary chain-case to its bracket. Model 120 has four separate steel rods.

90   THE BOOK OF THE PANTHER HEAVYWEIGHT

to ensure a gas-tight seal. The exhaust valve can readily be identified by discoloration. On 1938–63 598 c.c. engines (Model 100) both valve heads are of the same diameter, but on the 1959–66 645 c.c. engines (Model 120) the inlet valve has a larger diameter head than the exhaust valve. Its incorrect replacement is therefore impossible.

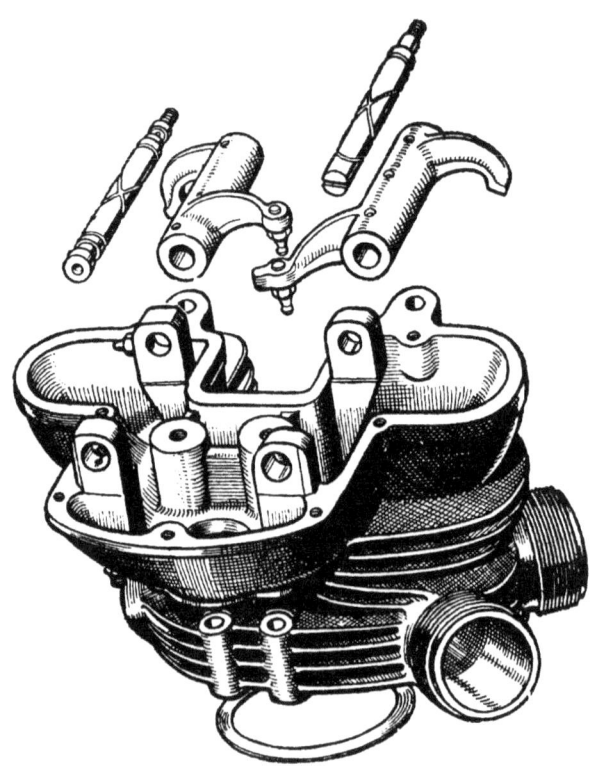

FIG. 44. SHOWING THE TWO-PORT CYLINDER HEAD WITH INTEGRAL ROCKER-BOX, AND SOME OVERHEAD ROCKER DETAILS
(*By courtesy of "Motor Cycle," London*)

6. Removing Cylinder Barrel. Removal of the cylinder barrel is normally not necessary when decarbonizing (see page 86; notes 5, 6), but can readily be effected if you wish to inspect the piston and piston rings.

After dismantling parts which get in the way, and then removing the cylinder head (see section 4) push or gently tap the long steel engine-rods further downwards, and then carefully withdraw the cylinder barrel from the piston. As the latter emerges from the mouth of the cylinder, steady it with one hand.

GENERAL MAINTENANCE

Never permit the light-alloy piston to fall sharply against the connecting-rod. If this happens, the skirt may become damaged or distorted. The piston has comparatively soft surfaces, and a vital role; treat it with the greatest respect.

When the cylinder barrel is removed, wrap a clean non-fluffy duster or rag round the exposed portion of the connecting-rod to cover completely the crankcase mouth. Any grit or metal object dropped accidentally into the crankcase may cause havoc when the engine is started. The removal of a foreign body is generally a most exasperating experience.

After the cylinder barrel is removed, see that the compressed

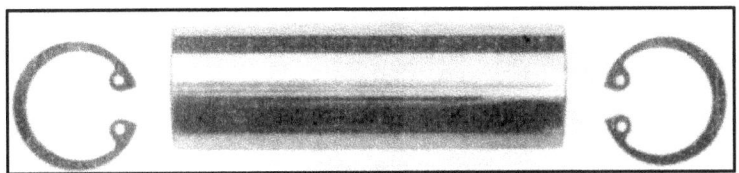

FIG. 45. THE GUDGEON-PIN AND CIRCLIPS
When removing the pin, circlip renewal is called for.

paper washer (see page 100) between the crankcase and cylinder barrel flange is not damaged. If it is damaged it must be renewed, otherwise some oil leakage is likely.

7. To Remove Piston. On all Panther engines the Hepolite flat-top piston is secured to the small-end of the connecting-rod by a $\frac{7}{8}$ in. diameter steel gudgeon-pin (see Fig. 45). The hollow pin is free to "float" in the small-end bush, and is a light-tap fit in the piston bosses at normal room temperature. End movement is controlled by two steel circlips which bed down into grooves at the outer ends of the piston boss bores. As the clearance between the gudgeon-pin and piston bosses is somewhat fine, removal of the pin is best effected with a gudgeon-pin removal tool (which presses it out) such as the Terry (see Fig. 46), or if not available with a hammer and a suitable drift.

With a small pair of snipe-nosed pliers very carefully remove the two circlips shown in Fig. 45 by inserting the pointed ends of the pliers into the circlip holes and squeezing the ends of each circlip towards each other until it is possible to withdraw the circlip from the piston-boss groove. Scrap the circlips after removal. It is unsafe to use them again as their temper may have become affected.

After removing both circlips, press out the hollow gudgeon-pin

92   THE BOOK OF THE PANTHER HEAVYWEIGHT

with a gudgeon-pin removal tool, or if not available, use a drift comprising a short length of brass or soft-metal bar with diameter slightly less than ⅞ in. If practicable, first warm the piston slightly.

When tapping the gudgeon-pin from one side always support the other side of the piston firmly, to avoid imposing any bending stress on the connecting-rod. As the gudgeon-pin emerges, note

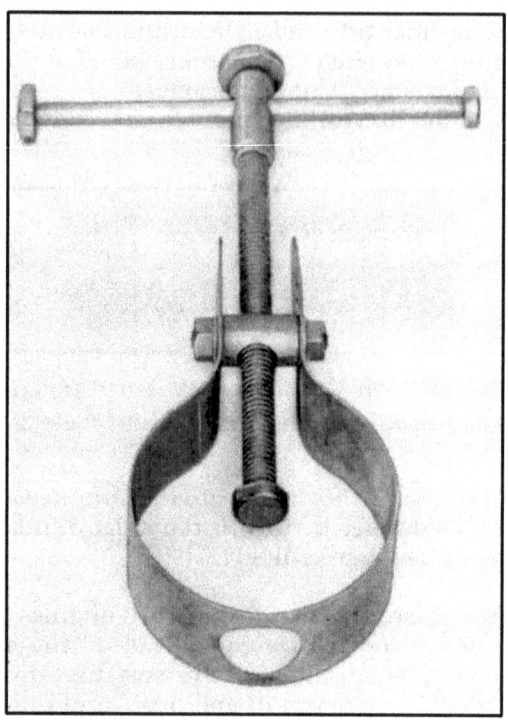

FIG. 46. A SUITABLE PROPRIETARY TOOL (THE TERRY) FOR REMOVING OR REPLACING A TIGHT GUDGEON-PIN

The tool shown has three pads for fitting different size gudgeon-pins.

its position relatively to the piston bosses because the gudgeon-pin should always be in the *same running position*.

Take the piston (see Fig. 47) off the connecting-rod; note its position, relatively to the rod. The piston laps out the cylinder in a certain manner, depending on various factors such as thrust, lubrication, etc. Consequently always replace the piston in the same position.

On many 598 c.c. Panther engines a slight "V" is formed inside the piston at the bottom of its skirt on the thrust (rear) side, and if the piston is always replaced with this "V" to the *rear*, no alteration in the running position of the piston is possible. Should there

GENERAL MAINTENANCE

be no "V" present, or decipherable, mark the bottom of the piston skirt (inside) with an appropriate "R" so as to show clearly the rear side.

8. Piston-ring Removal. When you go to the trouble of removing the piston consider removing the piston rings so that they and the grooves in which they fit may be thoroughly inspected and cleaned. Before removing the rings, however, make a careful visual inspection. The rings maintain compression, and

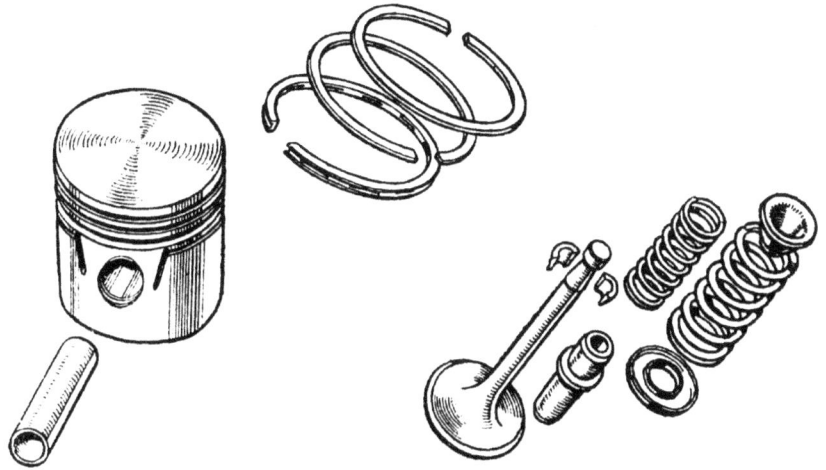

FIG. 47. 1952–66 SPLIT-SKIRT HEPOLITE PISTON, AND VALVE DETAILS

The bottom ring is the slotted oil-control ring which can be fitted either way up.

(*By courtesy of "Motor Cycle," London*)

must be full of springiness and quite free to move in their grooves, but not actually slack.

If a quick visual inspection shows that the compression rings are badly discoloured, and the piston-ring lands and piston skirt perhaps scorched also, probably one, or perhaps two, of the rings has become stuck in its groove, causing gas leakage. Look for evidence of the rings having become gummed-up and for the accumulation of carbon deposits which can generally be readily detected. Gummed-up rings must, of course, be removed, and substantial carbon deposits must be scraped from both the rings and their grooves.

If the piston rings appear to be perfect and carbon deposits not appreciable, it is probably best not to disturb the rings. Unnecessary ring removal is considered bad practice and can cause a temporary reduction in engine compression. But if in any doubt as to the condition of the piston rings, remove all three of them, so that a closer inspection of the rings and grooves can be made after thorough cleaning. The three rings are shown removed in Fig. 47.

9. Removal Procedure. The two plain compression-rings and the slotted oil-control ring are all very brittle, being made of cast-iron. The rings, especially the oil-control ring, are very easily broken if sprung out wider than about the diameter of the piston crown. Consequently extreme care must always be taken when removing the rings.

Undoubtedly the safest and most convenient method of removing (and fitting) the piston rings is that illustrated diagrammatically in Fig. 48. Insert three strips of thin sheet metal about 2 in. long and about ⅜ in. wide under the rings and equally spaced. Then gently ease the rings off one by one, starting with the top compression ring. As it is desirable to replace serviceable compression rings in their *original grooves*, put the rings aside so that they can be subsequently identified. Be particularly careful when removing the slotted oil-control ring, and on no account scratch or otherwise damage the lands between the rings. Scoring here can be very detrimental.

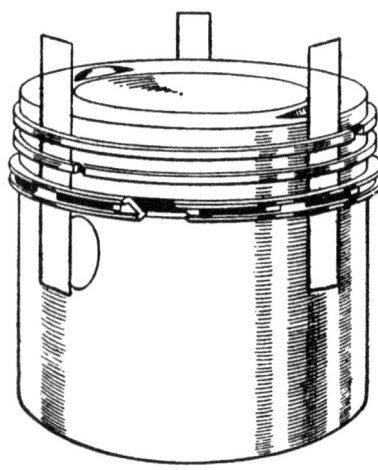

FIG. 48. THE SAFEST METHOD OF REMOVING AND FITTING THE PISTON RINGS

If the piston rings are badly gummed-up with sticky carbon deposits, it is advisable to immerse the piston head in a bath of paraffin for about 20 minutes to soften the deposits, before attempting to remove them. In extreme cases it may be necessary to remove the rings with a proprietary tool, or even to break them.

If a slight piston seizure occurs, probably some smearing of the aluminium alloy at the edges of the lands will prevent the rings springing out, thereby causing serious loss of engine compression. The appropriate remedy is to remove the barest amount of smeared metal with a *very fine* file, such as a nail file. An expert mechanic should do this. A very badly smeared piston, with generally some scoring, requires renewal.

10. Examining Cylinder and Piston. Hold the cylinder barrel up to the light and note the condition of its bore. It should have

GENERAL MAINTENANCE 95

a glossy surface all over for the distance traversed by the piston, and there should be no longitudinal scores or circumferential ridges present, unless a very big mileage has been covered. In this case wear can sometimes be felt as a distinct ridge near the upper end of the piston stroke.

A rebore is generally required when wear at the top of the bore reaches 0·010-0·015 in. Phelon & Moore, Ltd., can supply a piston and rings which are 0·020 in., 0·030 in. 0·040 in., and 0·060 in. oversize in diameter. To fit these a rebore to suit is called for, and reboring is best undertaken at the Panther factory or by rebore specialists.

Normally the cylinder and piston of a Panther engine remain serviceable for a very big mileage, after which some loss of compression and power may occur because of wear of the cylinder bore, piston, and rings.

Inspect the piston carefully for scorching or blackening of the skirt and ring lands, longitudinal scores, scratches, smearing, and other damage, especially in the vicinity of the piston ring lands. Inspect the piston-ring grooves for cleanliness (see section 13) and damage.

11. Inspecting and Cleaning Piston Rings. It is assumed the rings are removed (see section 8). To obtain good engine compression all three rings must, as previously stated, have good springiness, be quite free but not slack in their grooves, and be polished all round; their gaps must be of the correct size and equally spaced when the rings are in the cylinder bore.

If close inspection shows that the rings are bright all round, obviously they are making good circumferential contact with the cylinder bore and are fit for further service. If, however, the surfaces are found to be discoloured or scorched at some places, and this is not due to the rings having been stuck in the grooves, contact is poor and ring renewal is indicated. The same applies where there is vertical slackness of the rings in their grooves, or scratches on the outside of the rings.

Clean the inside faces and also the ends of the piston rings thoroughly (see section 13). Do not forget the slots in the oil-control ring (see Fig. 48). Piston rings are made to very fine limits and it is not generally wise to fit oversize diameter rings unless the piston is also renewed. When ring renewal is necessary, always fit genuine Panther spares which are guaranteed to be dimensionally correct.

12. Piston Ring Dimensions. The widths of the two compression rings and the slotted oil-control ring on all engines are $\frac{3}{32}$ in. and $\frac{5}{32}$ in. respectively. With a *new* piston the normal ring gap is 0·008–0·010 in. and rings should be renewed when the gap exceeds 0·015–0·020 in. The normal clearance on a new piston of each ring in its groove is 0·001 in., and the maximum permissible clearance is 0·003 in. New rings bed down within 2,000–3,000 miles, and the makers say that new standard-size rings can be fitted even when there is some wear of the cylinder bore.

After a very considerable mileage, or if some loss of compression occurs with the valves in good condition, check the gap between the ends of each piston ring. To do this push the ring squarely into the bore of the cylinder barrel with the aid of the piston, and then check the gap with a suitable feeler gauge. Should the gap prove to be outside the maximum permissible limit, fit a new ring, and again check the gap, which should then be correct. If it is not large enough, remove a little metal from *one* end of the ring with a file, so as to increase the gap to 0·008–0·010 in.

13. Scrape off all Carbon Deposits. The most satisfactory tool to use for scraping off carbon deposits is an old (blunted) wood chisel or a wide screwdriver, or else a proprietary scraper. For cleaning piston-ring grooves a suitable scraper can be made up by fitting a handle to a broken piece of piston ring ground at one end; a broken piece of hacksaw blade, or better still a proprietary groove scraper, can also be used.

It is always worth while decarbonizing the engine *thoroughly*, as carbon deposits form less readily on smooth surfaces. If heavy carbon deposits are found, apply a little paraffin to soften them.

If cylinder-barrel removal has not been undertaken, scrape carefully all the carbon from the piston crown, but *never use an abrasive on the piston.* This can have a most disastrous effect and, if it gets between the bore and piston, cause the piston to lap out the cylinder. Be most careful not to scratch the surface of the light-alloy piston.

If a vice is available, use it to hold the cylinder head by the overhead rocker bearings. If you have not a vice, stand the cylinder head with the rocker bearings resting on the bench or table.

Scrape off all carbon from the inside of the combustion chamber, not forgetting the sparking-plug hole. Chip off and remove all carbon from the valve ports, the vicinity of the valves,[*] and from the valve heads. Some *fine* emery cloth can be used to polish the combustion chamber, but if this is used, great care must afterwards be taken to remove completely every trace of the abrasive particles, using a rag damped in paraffin. On no account

[*] With the valves removed, be careful not to damage the faces of the valve seats. It is advisable to insert the valves temporarily while decarbonizing the inside of the combustion chamber.

meddle with the surface of the cylinder bore, even if locally blackened.

If the cylinder barrel and piston have been removed, scrape any carbon deposits (not often appreciable) from the inside of the piston. Remove all carbon from the top of the piston crown, but do not touch the skirt near the crown or elsewhere.

The piston rings have been referred to in section 11. The ring grooves also require attention. Clean the grooves very thoroughly but be careful not to damage the sides of the grooves. See that the holes in the groove for the oil-control ring (see Fig. 48) are unobstructed. After decarbonizing, clean all parts thoroughly with clean rags and paraffin. As regards the two Panther tubular-type silencers, note that these need not and cannot be dismantled for internal cleaning.

14. Grind-in Both Valves. Although Phelon & Moore, Ltd., advise removal, and if necessary grinding-in, of the valves each time the engine is stripped for decarbonizing, too frequent and excessive grinding-in is most undesirable. If the valves are making perfect contact with their seats, leave them alone. Excessive valve grinding can cause the valves to become "pocketed" in the seats. This obstructs the smooth flow of gas and reduces engine efficiency. Check valve guide wear (para. 15).

When both valves have been removed, clean their heads thoroughly, and also polish the valve stems with some *fine* emery cloth. When doing this, hold the emery cloth between the forefinger and thumb against the valve stem and move the cloth longitudinally up and down. After polishing both valve stems, grind-in each valve on to its seat with a good-quality grinding paste such as Richford's (coarse and fine grades are obtainable).

To grind-in an inlet or exhaust valve, lay the cylinder head on the bench. Then smear some *fine* grinding paste on the bevelled face of the valve, after first making sure that the valve and its seat are quite clean. If an exhaust valve and its seat faces are extensively pitted (as sometimes happens), it may be necessary to grind-in the valve with some *coarse-grade* paste before using the fine grade. Very severe pitting can only be dealt with by having the valve seat, and perhaps the valve also, refaced with a cutter having a cutting angle of 45 degrees.

With the valve inserted on its seat and grinding paste applied to the valve, oscillate the valve about a quarter of a turn backwards and forwards by means of a suitable valve holder, preferably a suction type. Maintain slight pressure between the valve and its seat during grinding-in, and lift the valve periodically and turn it to a new position. Continue with grinding-in until there is *a continuous matt ring* on the faces of both the valve and seat. Width of contact is not of much importance, provided such contact *is* perfect and continuous.

The inlet valve may require only one, or perhaps two, applications of valve grinding paste, but several may be needed to restore the exhaust valve to a gas-tight condition.

15. Remove All Traces of Grinding Paste. After grinding-in the valves, be sure that you remove *all* traces of grinding paste from the valve faces and valve seats. Clean both valves and seats with a clean rag and petrol or paraffin. Also draw a piece of clean cloth damped with paraffin through both valve guides. This will eliminate any dangerous abrasive particles which may possibly have entered the guide bores.

Check that the valve stems are still a good fit in their guides. With new valves and guides the minimum clearance provided is 0·0035 in. With worn parts there should be no appreciable slackness perceptible on fitting each valve in its guide and attempting to "rock" it sideways. Renew any badly worn guide or valve as excessive wear makes it impossible for the valve to seat properly, and this may damage its face.

16. Valve Spring Renewal. The valve springs generally show no signs of weakening until a big mileage has been covered.

Weakened valve springs interfere with quick, positive valve action and spoil efficiency. This weakening is reflected by a measurable decrease in the *free length* of the springs when removed.

New (inlet and exhaust) inner and outer valve springs (see Fig. 47) have a free length of $1\frac{13}{16}$ in. and $2\frac{1}{2}$ in. respectively. Renew any valve spring whose free length is found to be less than $\frac{3}{16}$ in. below the dimensions quoted above.

17. Testing the Connecting-rod Bearings. When the cylinder barrel and piston are removed for thorough decarbonizing, make a rough, but nevertheless reliable, check on the condition of the connecting-rod big-end and small-end bearings.

Turn the engine over so that the double-row roller big-end bearing is at bottom-dead-centre, and then by gripping the connecting rod and trying to pull and press it up and down, note whether there is more than the *barest amount* of "shake" present. There should not be, nor should any sideways "rock" be possible.

Replace the gudgeon-pin in the small-end bush and feel its fit (the clearance in a new bush is 0·0015 in.). Although the pin must be free to rotate, there should be no "shake" whatever.

18. Replace Valves and Valve Springs. Before replacing the valves and duplex valve springs it is advisable to wash the entire cylinder-head casting thoroughly in petrol or paraffin. See that all oil ducts are unobstructed (poke a piece of thin wire through them), and that the valve seats and valve guides are quite clean.

Smear some engine oil on the valve stems and then insert the inlet valve in the corresponding combustion-chamber seat. See that the exhaust valve (see page 90) is not accidentally fitted to the inlet valve seat.

Place the cylinder head (valves in position), with the fins uppermost and some wood packing inserted between the inlet valve head and the bench or table being used for assembly. Fit the duplex valve-spring (see Fig. 47). Replace the valve-spring lower collar, fit the inner and outer valve springs, replace the valve-spring upper collar, and finally replace the split collet.

To fit the split collet, compress the duplex valve-spring by pressing down firmly on the upper collar with both thumbs (using a spanner end to assist if necessary), or else by removing the packing from beneath the valve head and employing the Panther valve-spring compressor. Deal with the exhaust valve and its duplex spring similarly.

When replacing the split collets, see that they bed down properly on the valve stems. If any difficulty is experienced in getting the halves of a split collet to remain in position on the valve stem until the pressure on the valve spring is released, apply a little thick grease or petroleum jelly to the location for the split collet.

19. Testing the Valve Seals. Although not essential if the valves have been ground-in properly, it is considered by many good practice to test the valve seals by pouring some petrol through the ports and watching carefully for leakage past the valves. No moisture should be visible on the combustion-chamber side until a considerable interval has elapsed.

20. Fitting the Piston Rings. It is assumed that the ring grooves and rings have been thoroughly cleaned (see page 97), and that the holes in the bottom groove for the slotted oil-control ring (and the holes in the land below this ring) are quite clear. The piston rings may now be fitted. It is assumed that their gaps are within the permissible limits (see page 95).

Oil all three grooves and then fit in this order very carefully: (a) the oil-control ring, (b) the lower compression-ring, and (c) the upper compression-ring. It is advisable to fit the two compression rings in their original grooves; the oil-control ring (Fig. 48) may be fitted either way up. When fitting the rings, use three strips of thin sheet metal (about 2 in. × $\frac{3}{8}$ in.), as indicated in Fig. 48. By sliding the rings, one by one, over these strips the risk of breaking the rings, and scratching or damaging the piston lands and ring grooves is negligible.

21. To Replace Piston. The piston rings are assumed to have been fitted, and the piston to be thoroughly clean inside and out. Offer up the piston to the small-end of the connecting-rod; when doing this make absolutely sure that the piston is replaced with the "V" or "R" mark on the inside of the skirt to the *rear* (see page 92). Now oil the gudgeon-pin and insert it in its *original position* into the piston bosses and small-end bush.

As the gudgeon-pin is a light tap fit in the piston bosses it is desirable before fitting it, to heat the piston by immersing it in hot water or else by resting an electric iron on it. Then gently tap the gudgeon-pin home, using a suitable soft-metal drift (see page 92). Be careful to support the piston on the opposite side when doing this. Alternatively use a gudgeon-pin removal tool (see page 92).

When the gudgeon-pin has been forced right home, fit a *new* pair of gudgeon-pin circlips (see Fig. 45), holding each circlip and squeezing the ends together with a small pair of snipe-nosed pliers. Use a rotary motion to ensure that each circlip beds down snugly into its piston-boss groove.

Should a circlip spring out while the engine is running, it will probably ruin the cylinder bore completely. After replacing the piston and gudgeon-pin, cover up the piston and the mouth of the crankcase with a clean cloth pending the replacing of the cylinder barrel.

22. Replacing Cylinder Barrel. Before replacing the cylinder barrel wash out the cylinder bore with some paraffin. Avoid scratching the glossy surface of the bore, and see that the oil passage leading from the rear of the cylinder base to a point at the rear of the cylinder bore, is quite clear. Poke a piece of thin wire through this passage to make sure.

Also see that the cylinder-barrel spigot for the crankcase mouth, and the crankcase face for the cylinder barrel, are perfectly clean. Check that the cylinder-base washer is absolutely intact. Should this compressed-paper washer be in any way damaged, renew it immediately (to prevent oil leakage), and make sure that it is correctly positioned. It is advisable to stick the washer to the cylinder-barrel face with grease, or better still with a few dabs of jointing compound to ensure correct location.

On the 598, 645 c.c. engines the cylinder-base washer cannot be fitted the wrong side up and thereby obstruct the oil supply to the rear of the cylinder bore because on all cylinder-base washers two elongated holes are provided. The radiused extension must be next to the flange of the tappet guide and the cut-away opposite to the oil passage.

Smear some clean engine oil on the outside of the piston and the inside of the cylinder barrel, and then replace the cylinder barrel, after turning the engine over until the piston is at, or near. bottom-dead-centre. Make sure first, however, that the piston-ring gaps are spaced so that they are all 120 degrees apart.

Hold the cylinder barrel over the piston with one hand, and

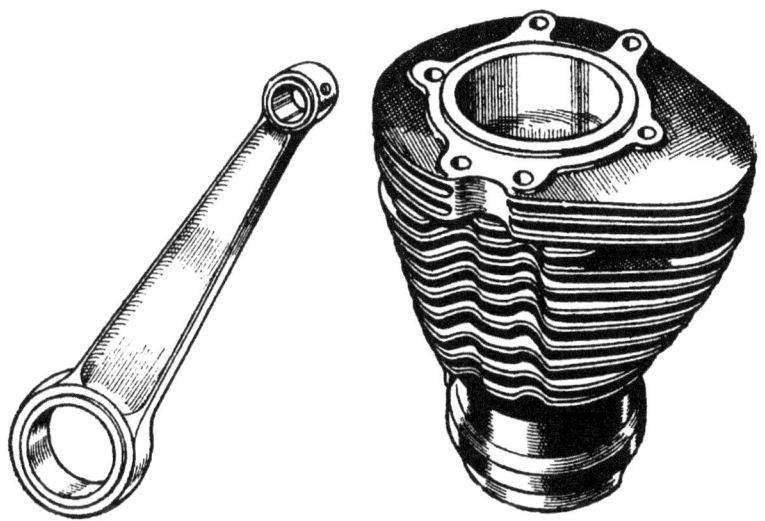

FIGS. 49, 50. SHOWING (LEFT) THE PANTHER CONNECTING-ROD AND (RIGHT) THE CYLINDER BARREL
(*By courtesy of "Motor Cycle," London*)

with the other offer up the piston, squeezing the rings together (without upsetting the spacing of their gaps) until the whole of the piston can be gently slid into the mouth of the cylinder barrel without friction, as the barrel is gradually lowered over the four long engine rods (two "U" rods, 1936-63), already tapped down.

Be careful not to impose any side stresses on the piston and/or connecting-rod during the replacement of the cylinder barrel, and see that the barrel spigot beds down into the crankcase mouth. No jointing compound is needed for the barrel-to-crankcase joint, but a new cylinder-base washer (if required) should be stuck to the cylinder-barrel face.

After the cylinder barrel has been fitted, push or tap up the four long steel engine-rods (or the two "U" rods) so that they protrude a short distance above the top face of the barrel.

23. Replace the Cylinder Head. It is assumed that the cylinder head has been thoroughly washed and that the valves have been replaced (see page 98). Wipe the top face of the cylinder barrel and the bottom face of the cylinder head quite clean, and place on the latter the cylinder-head copper gasket. The gasket must be clean and in perfect condition (see page 89).

Replace the cylinder head over the now slightly protruding long steel engine-rods. See that the head beds down squarely and snugly. No jointing compound is needed for the joint. Push or tap up the long engine rods to their full extent and fit to them the four nuts*; also fit to the inverted studs the two additional cylinder-head retaining nuts provided between the cylinder-head fins fore and aft. To fit the nuts to the cylinder-head studs, first raise the head slightly to enable the nuts to go between the fins and get a start on the threads.

Tighten all six cylinder-head retaining nuts, lightly first, and then firmly. To avoid distorting the cylinder-head casting, be careful to tighten the nuts evenly and diagonally.

24. Complete the Reassembly of Engine. In the reverse order of dismantling, fit the overhead rockers, the push-rods, and the push-rod cover tubes. Leave the cover tubes telescoped for the time being. Before replacing the rocker cover, wash it thoroughly in paraffin and renew the paper washer for the joint, if damaged. No jointing compound is required. When replacing the seven cover securing-screws, remember to fit the *longer* screw in the centre on the off side, otherwise the cylinder-head casting may be damaged.

Fit the top engine-mounting lugs to the cylinder head and tighten the four securing-screws very firmly. Replace the two steel bushes or cups, and replace the bolt securing the top engine-mounting lugs to the frame. Should any difficulty be experienced in fitting the two steel bushes or cups, this is caused by some slight spring in the frame. To overcome the trouble, insert a piece of $\frac{1}{2}$ in. diameter alignment rod or tube through one of the top engine-mounting lugs into the frame lug.

Raise the exhaust-valve lifter lever by turning the engine over until the exhaust cam raises the valve, and then reconnect the valve-lifter cable control to the valve-lifter lever by inserting the nipple. To assist its insertion, raise the lever with a small wire hook held just above the rocker-cover aperture. A useful tool which can be used instead is a 4 in. length of wheel spoke with one end bent to form a handle and the other end with two parallel flats filed on the sides of the spoke head.

---

* The two *larger* nuts must be replaced on the long engine rods which are on the push-rod (off) side of the engine.

GENERAL MAINTENANCE

Tighten the two screws securing the flange of the upper part of the push-rod cover tube to the cylinder head (fit a paper washer here, but no jointing compound). After checking that the tappet adjustment, and the adjustment of the exhaust-valve lifter (see page 84), are approximately correct, pull down the lower portion of the push-rod cover tube. Then with the "C" spanner (8, Fig. 39), secure the tube base to the tappet guide.

Replace the sparking plug (and copper washer), connect the h.t. lead, and also fit the carburettor after it has been well cleaned (see pages 25, 111). Insert the air and throttle slides into the mixing chamber of the carburettor and replace the mixing-chamber top. If necessary, adjust the two carburettor-control adjusters. Make sure that the slides operate freely and without excessive backlash. Replace the air filter (where provided).

25. Replace the Petrol Tank. First fit a rubber pad on top of each of the two tank front-support lugs. Also place a rubber pad over the hole on the *inside* of each vertical lug which is brazed to the rear of the tank.

Position the tank and rubber insulating pads correctly, and locate the tank by inserting the long horizontal stud through the holes in the tank and frame rear lugs. Tap this stud home from the end to which one nut is still attached and split-pinned; continue until an even amount of the stud projects at both ends. Fit the other bevelled washer (smaller than the front pair) and the castellated nut. But do not firmly tighten the nut and fix the split-pin, until you have replaced the two vertical bolts at the forward end of the tank.

To each of the two vertical bolts fit, first one of the larger plain steel washers, and then a rubber pad (see Fig. 43). The upper rubber pads are, of course, already in position. Next insert both the vertical bolts, together with the rubber pads and washers, through the holes in the tank front-support lugs, and screw the bolts home into the bosses on the tank.

Tighten both vertical bolts lightly and then with the appropriate spanners tighten these two bolts, and also the castellated nut on the rear horizontal stud, *moderately*. Excessive tightening must be avoided, otherwise the rubber insulating pads will be compressed and reduce their value as insulation against shocks.

Lock the castellated nut with a split-pin. It is also advisable to wire-lock the two vertical bolts at the front, using a single piece of wire inserted through the holes drilled in the bolt heads. Finally fit and tighten the union nuts securing the petrol pipe to the two tank-tap unions and the float-chamber union.

When tightening the petrol-pipe union nuts, do not forget to hold each tap hexagon with a spanner, otherwise its tank joint may be strained. Turn on the petrol to verify absence of leakage, and to prevent the float in the float chamber becoming damaged, through being "loose."

26. Change Oil and Clean the Filter. Whenever the engine has been decarbonized, change the oil in the sump and clean the gauze filter. If carbon deposits have become so substantial that they have to be removed by scraping, it is fairly certain that the engine oil circulating in the dirty engine has also become contaminated.

Instructions for changing the engine oil and removing and cleaning the gauze filter are given in Chapter III. Your mount is now ready for the road again.

27. Check Tappets After Warming Up the Engine. After assembling the engine, replacing the tank, and changing the oil, warm up the engine to its *normal working temperature* and after covering about 50 miles, check that the adjustment (see page 82) of both tappets is correct.

DECARBONIZING PROCEDURE—645 C.C. MODEL 120 ENGINE (1959-66)

On a Few Earlier Engines. As has been stated on page 85, para. 2, where hexagon spanner holds are *not* provided at the bottom of the engine rods a necessary preliminary to decarbonizing is to remove the complete engine from the frame (*see* later paragraph) after first removing the petrol tank, exhaust pipes, and silencers as described on pages 86-7. Then proceed with the stripping down, decarbonizing, valve grinding, and reassembly as described for the Model 100 engine on pages 87-104 (paras. 3-27).

On All Later Engines. Where hexagon spanner holds *are* provided at the bottom of the engine rods follow the stripping down, decarbonizing, valve grinding, and reassembly procedure described for the Model 100 engine on pages 86-104 (paras. 1-27).

Removing 645 c.c. Engine from Frame. The procedure required for removing the complete engine from the Model 120 frame is briefly as follows. First disconnect the engine controls, remove the outer portion of the oil-bath chain case and unscrew the engine sprocket nut after knocking back the locking washer. Then unscrew the clutch spring adjuster nuts, remove the clutch springs, and afterwards remove the clutch plate assembly. Next remove the clutch-centre nut after engaging top gear and locking the rear wheel by applying pressure on the rear brake pedal. After placing a suitable receptacle beneath the clutch

GENERAL MAINTENANCE

bearings to catch the rollers, withdraw the clutch centre, the spacer, the clutch sprocket, the bearings, and the engine sprocket (keyed to a parallel shaft).

Now remove the rear portion of the oil-bath chain case, place a suitable box beneath the engine crankcase, and press out the top engine bobbins. Then remove the rear unit fixing bolts which pass through the rear engine plates. The complete engine can then be removed from the frame.

VALVE TIMING AND TIMING CASE

The valve timing on Model 100 and 120 engines has been determined with extreme accuracy after entensive calculation and research by the makers. You can never improve on this timing.

To Ensure Correct Valve Timing. Three of the gears in the timing case are marked on assembly at the Panther factory. A dot system of marking is used for the gear teeth to facilitate correct re-meshing of the gears, and if the gears are always replaced with the dot marks correctly aligned, it is impossible to disturb the valve timing.

Normally it is unnecessary to check the timing by attaching a degree disc to the crankshaft, or by taking measurements on the piston stroke, to indicate the exact moments when the inlet valve opens and the exhaust valve closes (I.O. and E.C.).

To ensure that the valve timing is correct, it is only necessary to see that the engine pinion is kept meshed with the camwheel so that the single dot on the pinion aligns with one of the two dots on the camwheel, the other dot on the camwheel being aligned with one of the two dots on the intermediate gear housing the oil-pump plunger.

The second dot mark on the intermediate (oil-pump) gear is for aligning with the dot mark on the magneto driving-gear. Should the magneto, "dyno-mag," or "Magdyno" not be disturbed when removing the gears from the timing case (see below), it is only necessary to align the dot marks correctly to ensure the ignition timing being unaltered.

An Approximate Check on Timing. A rough check on the timing of the valves can be made by "rocking" the engine about the T.D.C. position an equal amount either side. The inlet valve should be observed to open, followed by the closing of the exhaust valve.

To Dismantle Gears in Timing Case. Dismantling is quite simple. First remove the foot gear-change lever to obtain easy

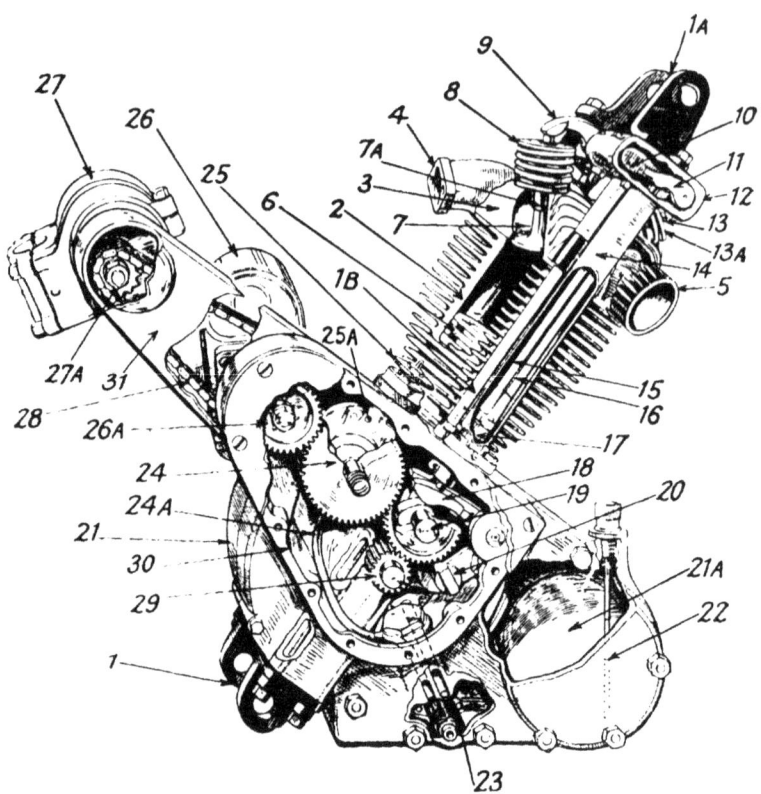

Fig. 51. Cut-away View of 598 c.c. O.H.V. Engine Showing Gear Train, etc.

The engine shown is a 1950 type with separate magneto, but subsequent engines are fundamentally similar (see Fig. 53).

1. Bottom engine-mounting lugs.
1A. Top engine-mounting lugs.
1B. Engine-mounting rod (one of 4). 2 "U" rods used 1936-63
2. Cylinder barrel.
3. Cylinder head.
4. Inlet port.
5. Exhaust port (off-side).
6. Aluminium-alloy piston.
7. Inlet valve.
7A. Inlet-valve guide.
8. Duplex inlet-valve spring.
9. Outer inlet-rocker arm.
10. Inner inlet-rocker arm.
11. Inner exhaust-rocker arm.
12. Rocker-box (integral with cylinder head, 1938 on).
13. Exhaust valve.
13A. Duplex exhaust-valve spring.
14. Telescopic push-rod cover tube.
15. Inlet push-rod.
16. Exhaust push-rod.
17. Tappet adjustment.
18. Exhaust cam follower.
19. Camwheel and camshaft (integral).
20. Decompressor inner-lever.
21. Engine crankcase.
21A. Oil-sump reservoir.
22. Dip-stick (modified, 1938 on).
23. Gauze filter (modified, 1938 on).
24. Intermediate gear, housing oil pump.
24A. Suction pipe from filter to oil pump.
25. Oil-pump regulator (omitted, 1938 on).
25A. Oil port (auxiliary).
26. Magneto ("Magdyno," 1951 on).
26A. Magneto driving-gear (modified, 1945 on).
27. Dynamo casing (1938-51).
27A. Dynamo driving-sprocket.
28. Dynamo driving-chain (1938-51).
29. Engine pinion.
30. Timing-case cover.
31. Dynamo chain-case (1938-51).

GENERAL MAINTENANCE

access. Next remove the eleven screws which secure the cover to the timing case, and carefully pull away the cover. Do not attempt to prise it off, and be careful not to lose the spring-loaded cap which holds the intermediate gear firmly against the spigot bearing (essential for the oil pump). Remove the intermediate gear and push out the oil-pump plunger.

With the engine turned so that both valves are closed, slacken off the tappets, and remove the camwheel and integral camshaft from its bush. To do this, it is not essential first to remove the two valve-cam followers and the decompressor inner-lever and tongue.

To remove the valve-cam followers (if desired) it is necessary to extract their bearing pin. The best way of doing this is to screw a $\frac{1}{4}$ in. diameter bolt into the threaded hole in the outer end of the pin. A nut should be fitted to the outer end of the bolt. Then tap on the inner face of the nut and the bearing pin comes away from the crankcase wall.

When removing the two valve-cam followers and the decompressor inner-lever, be careful not to lose the distance washer located *behind* the valve-cam followers.

To Assemble Gears in Timing Case. Assemble the gears, cam followers, etc., in the reverse order to that used for dismantling. Replace the two valve-cam followers* after first seeing that the distance washer is fitted *behind* them. Tap the bearing pin for the cam followers gently into position, but do not tap the pin too far home into the crankcase, otherwise the cam followers may bind. Also replace the decompressor inner-lever and its tongue.

Now raise the valve-cam followers and the tongue, and fit the camwheel and also the intermediate gear (complete with oil-pump plunger), so that the four timing dots on the gears are correctly aligned (see page 105). See that the decompressor tongue is *above* the thin cam, and resting on it.

Care must be taken when replacing the intermediate gear. See that the pump plunger (*D*, Fig. 12) is positioned in the gear-boss holes, and if necessary rotate the intermediate gear while replacing it, to enable the eccentrically fixed crankcase stud to register with the recess in the pump plunger.

Before replacing the timing-case cover, see that the spring and bearing cap for the intermediate gear are correctly fitted. The spring must be inside the cap and the solid end of the latter in contact with the centre of the intermediate gear. A blob of grease on the domed end of the pump plunger will facilitate replacement.

When replacing the timing-case cover and decompressor outer

* Before fitting the valve-cam followers, inspect the lower surfaces which contact the cams. If much wear is present, renew the followers.

lever, see that the faces of the self-aligning bearings are as square as possible and that the projection on the decompressor shaft is in a position similar to that of the slot cut for it in the end of the outer-lever shaft. Renew the paper washer if it is in any way damaged. No jointing compound is needed for this joint. Tighten the eleven cover-securing screws evenly and firmly.

A COMPLETE ENGINE OVERHAUL

If, after covering a very large mileage, the engine begins to show signs of wear and tear, indicated by poor performance and mechanical noise, get the engine completely overhauled. A complete overhaul is best undertaken by the makers or by George Clarke (Motors) Ltd., 73 New Park Road, Brixton, London, S.W.2. If you have considerable skill, some repair work may be attempted, but special tools and equipment are needed for most major repair operations.

For a complete overhaul, the engine must be removed from the frame, stripped down completely, and all parts closely inspected. All worn or damaged parts if found unserviceable must be repaired or renewed.

To Remove Model 100 Engine. First remove the petrol tank and also the exhaust pipe(s) and silencer(s) (see pages 86-7). Also disconnect the carburettor, exhaust-valve lifter controls; and the ignition-timing control (on pre-1947 and post-1950 models).

Remove both footrests, the rear-brake pedal, the primary-chain case cover, the primary chain, and the clutch sprocket. Remove the engine sprocket with an extractor. Then remove the rear half of the primary-chain case. Remove the three $\frac{3}{8}$ in. diameter bolts passing through the two engine plates and the crankcase, also the top fixing-bolt and the rubber bushes which pass through the steering head.

On removing the last bolt which secures the engine, insert some suitable packing beneath the engine sump to avoid any risk of the engine falling out of the frame as it is freed.

To Remove Model 120 Engine. See instructions on page 104.

THE "MONOBLOC" CARBURETTOR

An Amal two-lever "Monobloc" carburettor is fitted to all 1955-66 Model 100 and 120 Panthers. This flange-fitted semi-automatic instrument differs from the earlier standard Amal carburettor dealt with in Chapter II, but its general functioning is similar.

The "Monobloc" carburettor (see Fig. 52) includes these features: a horizontal float-chamber made integral with the body of the carburettor; a float-chamber needle of moulded nylon; a hinged float; a top petrol feed; a needle-jet with "bleed" holes, giving two-way compensation; and a pilot jet which can be readily removed for cleaning.

Tuning "Monobloc" Carburettor. If you wish to tune the carburettor, follow the instructions given on pages 21-5 for tuning the standard Amal instrument. With the "Monobloc" carburettor it is, of course, possible to adjust the throttle-stop screw without first having to slacken a lock-nut (which is omitted).

In practice it is seldom necessary to interfere with the carburettor except perhaps to make a slow-running adjustment by means of the pilot-air adjusting screw and the throttle-stop screw (shown at (22) and (20) in Fig. 52). Aim at obtaining the best tick-over (with the throttle twist-grip shut right back, the air lever wide open, and the ignition lever three-quarters advanced) with a mixture bordering on the weak side. The engine should be on the point of spitting-back after starting from cold. "Rev" the engine up and down several times (while at rest and riding) after making a slow-running adjustment, and note if the exhaust is crisp, with no "flat spots," as the twist-grip is turned.

It is essential to combine good tick-over with good acceleration.

With regard to the paragraph (page 24) headed "Pilot Jet Obstructed," if an obstruction occurs in the pilot jet of a "Monobloc" carburettor (see Fig. 52), remove the pilot-jet cover nut (18) and unscrew the pilot jet (19). The jet can then be thoroughly cleaned in petrol and blown through.

"Monobloc" Carburettor Setting (1955 Onwards). The correct setting (which should not be altered without good reason) for the Amal, type 376/30 "Monobloc" carburettor is as follows—
    Main Jet: size 280 (250 on 1956-7 Model 100).
    Pilot Jet: size 30.
    Throttle Valve: 376/3½ (389/3 on Model 120).
    Needle Position: No. 3 (middle groove).

Dismantling "Monobloc" Carburettor. First turn off both petrol taps, and disconnect the petrol feed-pipe banjo union from the float chamber (see Fig. 52) by removing the banjo bolt (8). Where an air filter is fitted, remove this from the carburettor air-intake. Remove both nuts securing the carburettor flange to the inlet flange screwed to the inlet port, and unscrew the knurled mixing-chamber cap (2) on top of the mixing chamber. Remove the complete carburettor, and at the same time withdraw the air and throttle valves (3) and (26). Do not detach the slides unless it is necessary to renew the slides or control cables.

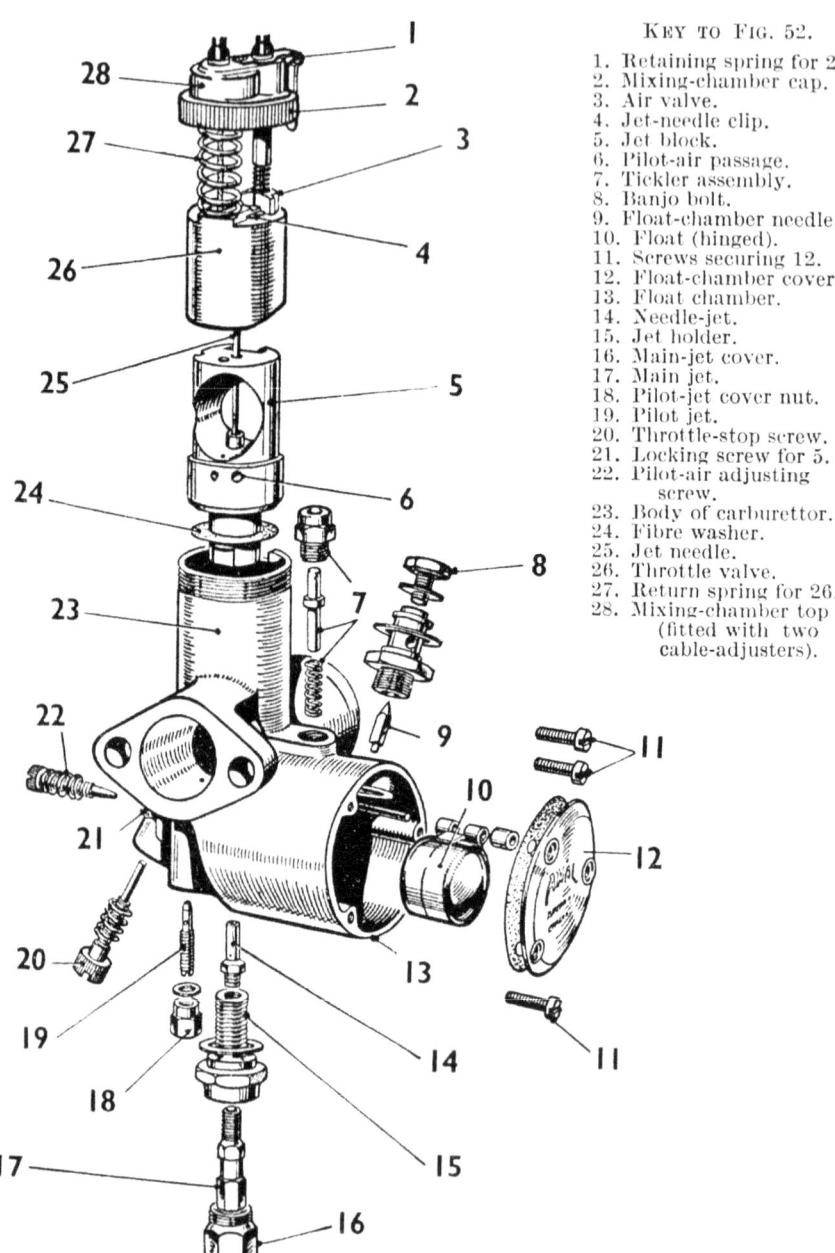

KEY TO FIG. 52.

1. Retaining spring for 2.
2. Mixing-chamber cap.
3. Air valve.
4. Jet-needle clip.
5. Jet block.
6. Pilot-air passage.
7. Tickler assembly.
8. Banjo bolt.
9. Float-chamber needle.
10. Float (hinged).
11. Screws securing 12.
12. Float-chamber cover.
13. Float chamber.
14. Needle-jet.
15. Jet holder.
16. Main-jet cover.
17. Main jet.
18. Pilot-jet cover nut.
19. Pilot jet.
20. Throttle-stop screw.
21. Locking screw for 5.
22. Pilot-air adjusting screw.
23. Body of carburettor.
24. Fibre washer.
25. Jet needle.
26. Throttle valve.
27. Return spring for 26.
28. Mixing-chamber top (fitted with two cable-adjusters).

FIG. 52. EXPLODED VIEW OF AMAL "MONOBLOC" CARBURETTOR (ALL 1955-66 MODEL 100, 120 PANTHERS)

(By courtesy of B.S.A. Motor Cycles, Ltd.)

GENERAL MAINTENANCE

Referring to Fig. 52, stripping-down the carburettor is quite straightforward. To remove the jet needle (25), withdraw the jet-needle clip (4) from the top of the throttle valve (26).

To obtain access to the hinged float (10), remove the three screws (11) securing the cover (12) to the float chamber (13). Lift out the hinged float and withdraw the moulded-nylon needle (9). Lay both aside for cleaning.

The float-chamber vent is incorporated in the tickler assembly (7), and the top-feed union houses a filter element of fine gauze which is readily accessible for cleaning, when the banjo union is disconnected.

To remove the main jet (17), remove the main-jet cover (16) and unscrew the main jet (17) from the jet holder (15). The needle-jet (14) can now also be unscrewed from the jet holder. Remove the jet block locking-screw (21) located to the left of and slightly below the pilot-air adjusting screw (22). Then push or tap out the jet block (5) through the larger end of the carburettor body (23). To remove the pilot jet (19) it is only necessary to remove the pilot-jet cover nut (18) and unscrew the pilot jet.

Cleaning "Monobloc" Carburettor. Wash all carburettor components thoroughly clean with petrol and blow through the various ducts and passages to make sure that they are quite clear. Avoid using a fluffy rag for drying purposes. Pay special attention to the pilot-air passage (6). Carefully remove all impurities from the float chamber, and do not forget to clean the detachable pilot jet and the filter gauze inside the top-feed union for the float chamber.

Inspecting "Monobloc" Components. If the carburettor has been in service for an appreciable period, inspect the following—

1. THE FLOAT CHAMBER. Examine the components very carefully. Check that the joint faces of the float-chamber cover and the float chamber are not bruised or damaged, and that the joint washer is sound, otherwise some difficulty may be experienced in maintaining a petrol-tight joint after assembly. The vent in the tickler assembly must be unobstructed, and the float in perfect condition. Clean the moulded-nylon needle very thoroughly, and be careful not to damage it.

2. THE THROTTLE VALVE. Test the valve for good fit in the mixing chamber. If excessive play exists, it is advisable to renew the slide immediately. See that the new slide has the correct amount of cut-away.

3. THE JET-NEEDLE CLIP. Note the remarks under this heading on page 25.

4. THE JET BLOCK. Before tapping this home in the carburettor body, verify by blowing that the pilot air passage (shown at (6) in

Fig. 52) is clear, and check that the fibre seal for the jet block is in sound condition.

5. THE CARBURETTOR FLANGE. Examine this for truth with a straight-edge. Distortion sometimes occurs, and this may cause an air leak. If the flange is slightly concave, grind or rub down the face with some emery cloth laid on a surface plate until it is dead flat and smooth. See that the heat-resisting joint washer is in perfect condition.

Assembling "Monobloc" Carburettor. Assemble the instrument in the reverse order of dismantling. Referring to Fig. 52, screw home the pilot jet (19) and the pilot-jet cover nut (18), not omitting to replace its washer. Push or tap home the jet block (5), with fibre washer (24), through the large end of the carburettor body (23). Then fit the jet block locking-screw (21). Screw the needle-jet (14) into the jet holder (15) and screw the latter into the jet block, after checking that the washer for the holder is sound. Next screw the main jet (17) into the jet holder and replace the main-jet cover (16).

Replace the moulded-nylon needle (9) in the float chamber (13), and fit the hinged float (10) with the *narrow side* of the hinge *uppermost*. Afterwards fit the float-chamber cover (12) and secure by means of the three screws (11). Renew the "O" washer.

If previously removed, attach the jet needle (25) to the throttle valve (26) and secure with the jet-needle clip (4), making sure that the clip enters the correct groove (see page 109).

Position the carburettor-flange washer and offer up the carburettor to the inlet-port flange, after easing the air and throttle slides (3) and (26) down into the carburettor body (23). When easing the throttle valve home, make certain that the tapered jet-needle (25) really enters the centre hole in the jet block (5). Secure the carburettor firmly and evenly by means of the two bolts, and then tighten down the mixing-chamber cap (2). Check that the throttle works freely when the cap is firmly tightened down.

Finally replace the air filter (if provided) and reconnect the twin petrol pipes by tightening the banjo bolt (8) on top of the float chamber (13). Before replacing the banjo, however, turn on the petrol for a second and observe whether it flows freely from the lower end of the pipe.

AIR FILTERS

The Vokes Filter (Pre-1956). A Vokes "oil-dip" type circular air filter is fitted to many pre-1956 Model 100 Panthers. The filter assembly is attached by an elbow to the carburettor air-intake.

GENERAL MAINTENANCE

About every 1,500-2,000 miles remove the outer cap (secured by one screw) from the filter assembly and withdraw the three-ply element. It is quite unnecessary to remove the complete filter assembly. Inspect the filter element for any signs of damage. Normally it is advisable to renew the three-ply element only about every 10,000 miles. Having removed the element, wash it thoroughly in petrol, allow to dry, and afterwards submerge it in thin, clean engine oil (grade: about SAE 20) for a few minutes. Allow all surplus oil to drain off for about 15 minutes, and replace the filter element. When doing this be most careful to locate the two felt sealing-washers correctly. At no point must the ends of the three-ply element and protective sheet-metal rings overlap the felt washers on either their inner or outer peripheries. After replacing the element fit the outer cap and tighten the central fixing-screw securely.

The Panther Filter (1956-66). The filter fitted to Model 100 and 120 subsequent to 1955 is of the demountable type. It employs an element of generous proportions, made of woven yarn and fine wire. To dismantle the filter assembly, remove it from the motor-cycle; unscrew the nut on the right-hand side of the petrol tank rear fixing-bolt, remove the filter fixing-bolt, when the element, complete with all metal fittings, will come away. Then wash the filter element in petrol or paraffin, oil the element and replace.

The yarn from which the element is partly woven absorbs large quantities of oil, and it is therefore inadvisable to apply thick oil to the filter element after washing it. Dip the element in a light upper-cylinder lubricant such as Redex and allow all surplus oil to drain off before replacing the element. It should normally be sufficient to clean and oil the filter element at intervals of approximately 10,000 miles. In dusty or sandy areas, however, attention may be needed about every 5,000 miles.

MAINTENANCE OF CYCLE PARTS

Do not neglect the cycle parts. Their maintenance is almost as important as that of the engine.

Note the advice given at the beginning of this chapter concerning the forwarding of parts to the makers or authorized Panther dealers.

You Will Want These Items. The following items will be found desirable for maintenance: a can of paraffin, a stiff brush for removing dirt from the lower parts of the motor-cycle, a tin of summer-grade engine oil (for the gearbox), some suitable oil

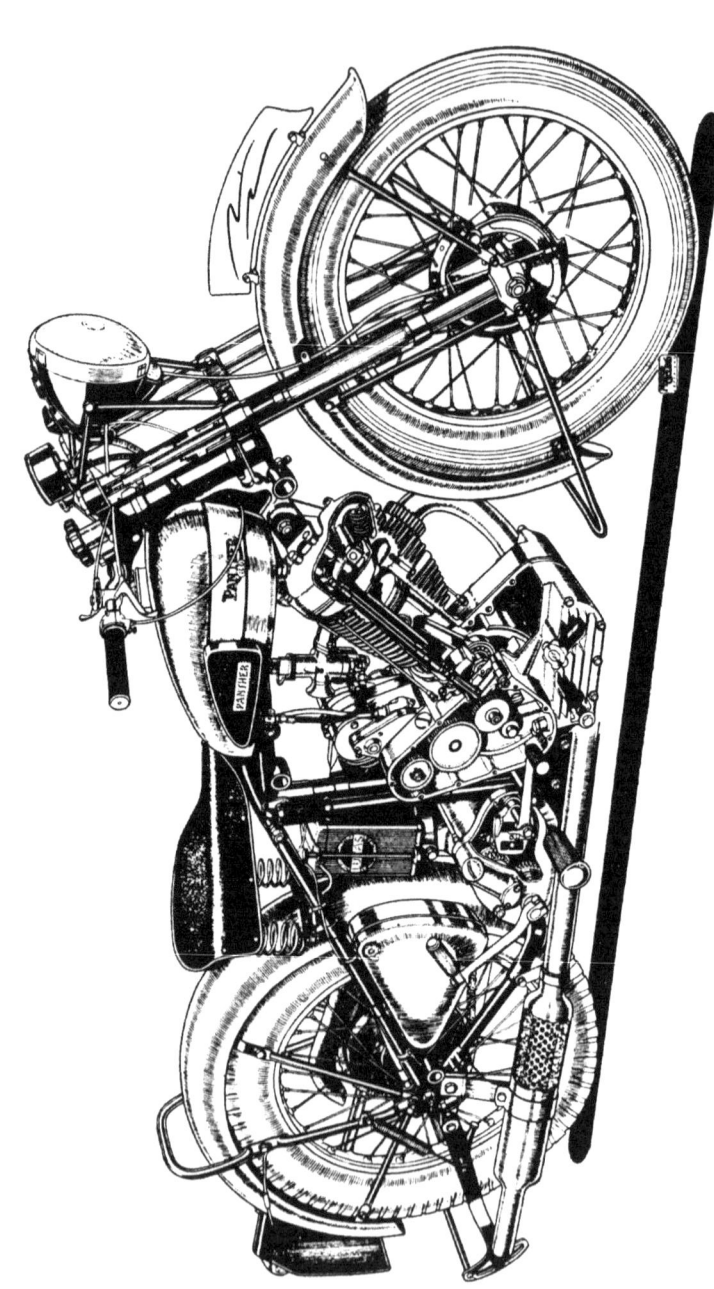

Fig. 53. Cut-away View of Earlier Model 100 with Rigid Frame
(*By courtesy of "Motor Cycling."*)

GENERAL MAINTENANCE

(see pages 117, 40) for topping-up 1954-66 Panther, or 1947-53 Panther-Dowty "Oleomatic," front forks, a canister of light grease (see page 39) for use with the grease gun, a tyre-pressure gauge, a hydrometer for checking the specific gravity of the battery electrolyte (see page 64), and a receptacle for draining the gearbox.

The following are needed for cleaning purposes: some jars or dishes for washing parts in, some non-fluffy rags, two chamois leathers, a sponge and pail (if no hose is available), some soft dusters, preferably of the Selvyt type, a tin of polish such as "Karpol" for the enamelled parts, and a tin of good hand cleanser such as "Swarfega."

Tools You Will Need. The Panther tool kit shown in Fig. 40 (excluding the engine maintenance tools 4, 5, and 8) are sufficient for all routine maintenance, stripping-down, and assembly, but purchase a good chain-rivet extractor and a box of spare chain links.

Maintenance of Tyres. Check the tyre pressures weekly with a gauge such as the "Holdtite," Dunlop pencil-type No. 6, Romac, or the Schrader No. 7750. For solo work 19 × 3·25 in. front and rear tyres should be inflated to 18 and 23 lb. per sq. in. respectively. On 1951 and subsequent models with 19 × 3·50 in. rear tyre, the correct rear pressure (solo) is 18 lb. per sq. in.

If a sidecar is attached, pump up the front and rear tyres (19 × 3·25 in.) to 18 lb. per sq. in. and 28 lb. per sq. in. respectively. On 1951-66 models with 19 × 3·50 in. rear tyre, the rear tyre pressure (with sidecar) should be 25 lb. per sq. in. The correct pressure for the sidecar tyre (all models) is 16 lb. per sq. in.

About once a year inspect the valve cores of the tyres. Periodically examine the treads and remove small stones or flints; fill up with some stopping compound. Use auto-vulcanizing patches for tyre repairs; when fitting tyres remember that wired-on type beads are non-stretchable. White spots on a cover (near the bead) must be located so that the valve is mid-way between them. On a sidecar outfit keep the wheels in correct alignment (see page 131). Always carry a good tyre-repair outfit.

Your Lighting Set. For full maintenance instructions, see Chapter V.

Correct Lubrication of Cycle Parts. This is fully dealt with in Chapter III. Attend to the lubrication matters referred to on pages 37-43.

Keep Your Panther Clean. Neglect of the enamelled and chromium-plated cycle parts will soon cause rusting and the machine will become unattractive-looking. Never leave it soaking wet over-night. If you have no time for thorough cleaning in wet weather, grease the machine all over before use. For removing filth from the lower part of the gearbox and machine, use a stiff brush and paraffin.

Cleaning the Enamel. Do not attempt to remove caked mud by trying to rub or brush it off when dry, but carefully soak it off, with a hose if available. Be careful not to direct a stream of water on to vulnerable parts. If a hose is not to hand, use a pail of water and a sponge for soaking off mud.

After removing all dirt and mud, dry the enamelled parts with a chamois leather; afterwards polish the surfaces with soft dusters and a good proprietary polish such as "Karpol."

Be Careful with Chromium. Never use ordinary liquid metal polish or paste to clean chromium-plated parts. Special chromium-cleaning compound can safely be used, but too frequent cleaning with this is not advised.

To remove tarnish (salt deposits), it is best to clean the surfaces regularly with a damp chamois leather and then polish them with a soft duster.

To Reduce Tarnishing. It is a good plan during the winter to wipe all chromium-plated surfaces with a soft cloth dipped in a proprietary preparation for reducing tarnishing. An excellent such preparation is "Tekall."

Maintenance of Panther Front Forks (1954 Onwards). The Panther oil-damped telescopic front-forks are of sturdy design and require very little maintenance. On 1956-66 models each fork leg incorporates an internal rubber dust-excluding ring of hard synthetic material. Eventually this ring may become dry and cause some artificial stiffness of fork action. It is also possible that after much riding in wet weather a slight squeak may be heard while the forks are in action. The remedy in either case is to squirt a small amount of oil through the hole provided in the cover-tube of each fork leg. The hole faces forward near the base of the cover-tube. New Panther front forks have somewhat small bearing clearances and the forks may be found a little stiff during the preliminary running-in period. All stiffness, however, normally disappears after covering 5,000 miles. Should stiffness persist after completing 5,000 miles, you are advised to drain and replenish the fork legs. Do this at 10,000 mile intervals.

Remove the drain plug from the foot of each telescopic fork leg and allow the oil to drain out. To ensure complete draining, work the forks up and down several times. Next place suitable packing

GENERAL MAINTENANCE 117

beneath the frame so as to raise the forks sufficiently to enable the front wheel to clear the ground when the fork legs are fully extended. Now remove the filler plug from the top of each fork leg and, using a funnel, pour in about ⅓ pint (¼ pint, 1956 onwards) of *winter grade* engine oil (see page 32). This should be done with the fork legs *fully extended*. Replace the copper washer and filler plug on top of each leg. Then remove the packing from beneath the engine and work the forks up and down several times. Should the fork action seem excessively stiff, drain a small and equal quantity of oil from each fork leg after covering about 100 miles. It is important to avoid running with insufficient oil in the fork legs, otherwise bottoming is liable to occur when running on rough roads or when the machine is heavily loaded. It is rarely necessary to dismantle the forks, but should it be necessary to renew the upper or lower bearings of the legs (after a very big mileage) you will find the necessary instructions included in the Panther Maintenance Manual supplied by the makers with each new machine.

Maintenance of the Panther-Dowty Front Forks. 1947-53 Panthers have Panther-Dowty "Oleomatic" front forks which are air-sprung and oil-damped. Very occasional inflation and adjustment to load may be necessary, but generally not until after a very large mileage.

The inflation valve (see Fig. 18) has a special core provided with oil-resisting rubber seatings. Never substitute for a genuine Dowty valve core a normal tyre-valve core, or you may destroy the natural rubber seatings.

A loading indicator (see Fig. 18) is included on the front of each lower sliding fork-tube. Each indicator comprises a *red dot*. The forks are correctly inflated for load when with the rider (and the passenger) seated, the *bottom edges of the shrouds are exactly aligned with the loading indicators*. The loading must be adjusted to suit solo riding, pillion riding, or sidecar driving.

To obtain correct inflation, first slightly over-inflate the telescopic forks by removing the dust cap from the inflation valve (Fig. 18) and pumping up with a tyre pump. Inject only a small amount of air. Now if you are a soloist, sit astride the saddle (with pillion passenger, if normally carried) and balance your mount from a convenient support.

If you own a sidecar outfit, get the whole "crew" aboard. Then depress the stem of the inflation valve and release air in small quantities until the bottom edges of the shrouds are observed to be in exact alignment with the two loading indicators (red dots). Afterwards replace the dust cap and screw it down securely.

If "bottoming" occurs while riding, even though the forks have been carefully inflated to load as just described, top-up the forks with suitable oil. Topping-up, greasing, and refilling the "Oleomatic" front forks are described in Chapter III. For steering-head adjustment, see page 124.

If Air Leakage Occurs (1947-53). If your Panther 100 has been idle for long, it may be found that the "Oleomatic" front forks have become deflated because the oil seals have become dry. When you attempt to reinflate the front forks you may find that the air is not held.

Remove the two filler plugs shown at *A* in Fig. 18, replenish each fork leg with a little fresh oil (see page 40), replace the two filler plugs, and inflate the front forks as just described. Then "bounce" the front forks vigorously several times to spread the oil.

Maintenance of Front Forks (Girder Type). For advice on lubrication, see Chapter III.

Some side play may gradually develop in the steering head and fork links. For the appropriate adjustment, see page 124.

Check Nuts and Bolts Regularly for Tightness. Forestall trouble by periodically checking all important nuts, bolts, and screws for tightness. See that the exhaust system and the equipment does not become loose, and that the wheel-spindle securing nuts are tight.

On 1947-53 models pay special attention to the nuts and screws on the "Oleomatic" front forks. See that the steering-pad bolt is kept firmly tightened, or you may find that the alignment of the forks becomes faulty.

Gearbox Maintenance. For instructions on replenishing and topping-up the 1938-66 Burman four-speed gearboxes, see page 37. Apart from regularly attending to gearbox lubrication and making clutch adjustments when necessary, you will find that the gearbox needs no further attention for a very big mileage. Then it may be desirable to have the gearbox stripped down and thoroughly overhauled. (See note on page 124 re: Burman gearbox overhauling).

To Adjust Handlebars. See page 3.

Footrest Adjustment. See page 3.

To Adjust Foot Gear-change Position. See page 3.

Keep the Brakes Efficient. Keep both brakes adjusted so that they will give even, prompt, and powerful braking. To obtain the best results, the adjustment of both brakes should be such

GENERAL MAINTENANCE

that with the brake lever or pedal released, the brake-shoe linings are almost in contact with the brake drums.

Brake linings gradually wear and an adjustment becomes necessary. Take up any excessive slackness in the control. Finger adjustment is provided for both brakes on 1938-46 Panthers, but on the 1947 and later machines with Panther-Dowty or Panther front forks a spanner must be applied to the hexagon-headed adjuster and lock-nut to make a front brake adjustment.

On 1956-66 spring-frame models with quickly-detachable wheels having full-width light-alloy hubs, each brake shoe operating-lever is secured to the shoe-operating cam spindle by fine serrations, and a wide range of adjustment of the angle of the brake-shoe operating lever is therefore possible. Always adjust the angle to give optimum leverage.

If some oil gets inside the brake drums on to the brake linings remove the brake shoes and clean their linings thoroughly with some petrol. Harshness in brake action can often be cured by filing down each brake lining for about 1 in. from each end. New brake linings have the rivet holes already drilled. No adjustment is provided on the brake shoes themselves.

Do Not Interchange Brake Shoes. It is not advisable to interchange the brake shoes fitted to the *same* brake cover-plate. It is impossible to interchange the front and rear-brake shoes (and associated parts).

Correct Chain Tension is Essential. Always keep a watchful eye on primary and secondary chain tension; immediately adjust where necessary.

Brand new chains stretch appreciably; remedy excessive whip immediately. When adjusting see that the chain is not tightened excessively.

To Retension Primary Chain (1938 Onwards). The primary chain runs in an oil-bath chain case, and therefore stretches somewhat less quickly than does the more exposed secondary chain. Occasionally (say, every 2,000 miles) check the tension of the primary chain and retension the chain if necessary. Always remember that the secondary chain will need an adjustment, if the primary chain is retensioned.

To check the tension, remove the inspection cover from the oil-bath chain case and with the fingers check the whip (total up-and-down movement) of the chain. Turn the engine and transmission over with the kick-starter and check the tension at several points along the chain run.

With the chain in its tightest position the whip* should be not less than ⅜ in. and should not exceed about ½ in. with the chain in its slackest position. If the chain and sprockets are not badly worn, the whip should be uniform throughout the length of the chain. The gearbox is pivot-mounted at the top and can be swung backwards to take up chain stretch.

Referring to Fig. 55, loosen the nuts on the gearbox top and bottom mounting-bolts A, B. Slacken the top nut about one turn, and the bottom nut about two turns. Also slacken the lock-nuts

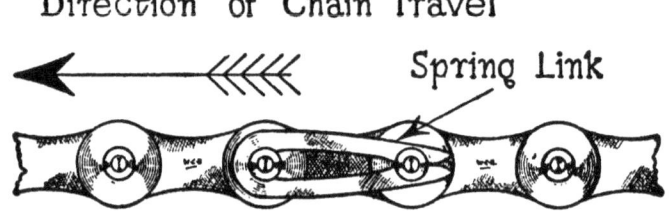

Fig. 54. Always Fit the Spring Link like this when Connecting a Primary or Secondary Chain

To facilitate connecting the chain, join its two ends when positioned close together on the clutch sprocket. Renew a chain when stretch exceeds ¼ in. per foot.

D, E which lock the two primary-chain adjuster screws C, F. Then to swing the gearbox backwards about its top pivot-bolt, unscrew the rear adjuster-screw F a number of turns and screw home the front adjuster-screw C until a correct chain whip of ⅜-½ in. is obtained. Afterwards screw home the rear adjuster screw to secure the gearbox firmly in its new position; do not forget to retighten firmly the adjuster screw lock-nuts and the nuts on the gearbox mounting-bolts.

IMPORTANT NOTE. It is extremely important before attempting to pivot the gearbox backward or forward first to slacken the adjuster screw F or C (Fig. 55) respectively. Failure to do this is likely to strip the adjuster-screw threads in the gearbox casing, and the makers emphasize this point.

To Retension Secondary Chain (1938 Onwards). The secondary chain stretches rather more quickly than the primary chain. Check it for tension regularly (say, every 1,000 miles) and always *after* retightening the primary chain.

* Where a sidecar outfit is concerned, to prevent chain rattle, slightly less whip is desirable than in the case of a solo mount.

To check chain tension, verify the whip (total up-and-down movement) mid-way between the gearbox and rear-wheel sprockets. With the foot gear-change lever in neutral turn the rear wheel over and verify the whip with the chain in a number of positions. When the chain is in its tightest position the whip should be not less than ½ in. and nowhere exceed ¾ in. (see also below).

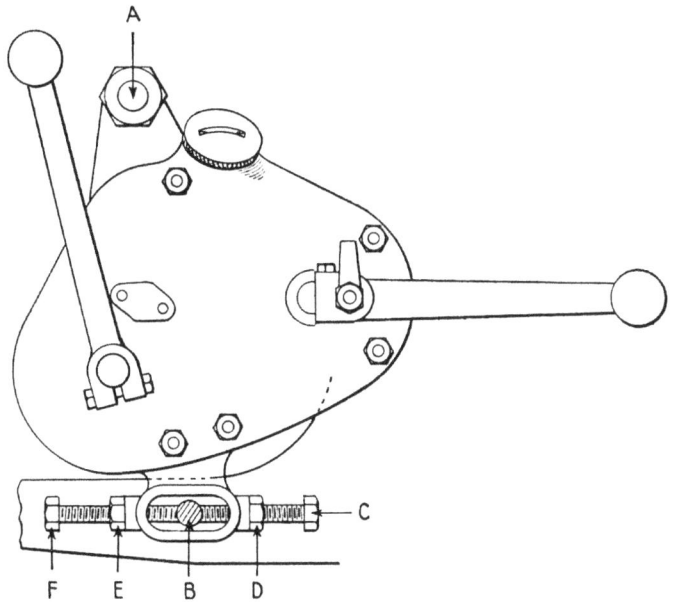

Fig. 55. Provision for Primary-chain Adjustment (1938 onwards)

A. Gearbox top-mounting (pivot) bolt.
B. Gearbox bottom-mounting bolt.
C. Front adjuster-screw for chain.
D. Lock-nut for C.
E. Lock-nut for F.
F. Rear adjuster-screw for chain.

On all machines prior to 1956 a cam adjustment for the rear-wheel position is provided, and this ensures permanent rear-wheel and secondary-chain alignment.

To tighten the chain (1938–55), loosen both rear-wheel spindle nuts and, with a spanner applied to the squared end of the wheel spindle, turn the spindle and the two eccentric cams fixed to it as indicated in Fig. 56. This will push the rear wheel backwards until the correct chain whip is obtained. While retensioning the chain always see that the two cams are hard up against the pegs fixed in the frame. Finally tighten the rear-wheel spindle nuts securely and again check the chain tension. See that all spring links are fitted with the open end facing *away from* the direction of chain movement.

On 1956-66 models with "swinging arm" rear suspension and quickly-detachable rear wheel, a cam adjustment for chain tension is not provided. The correct chain tension is such that with the chain in its tightest position there is a total up-and-down movement at the centre of the lower chain run of $\frac{1}{2}$-$\frac{3}{4}$ in., with the motor-cycle off its centre stand. To retension a secondary chain, first slacken off the spindle nut on the off side and also loosen the

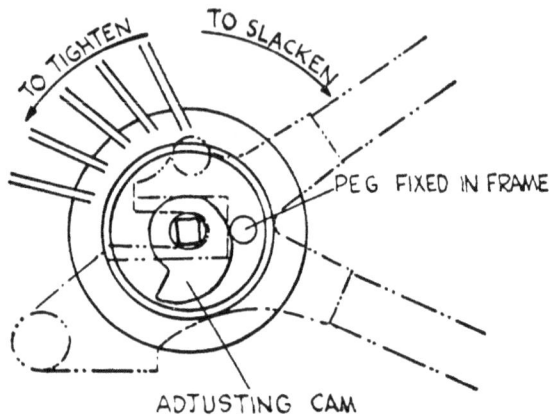

Fig. 56. To Retension Secondary Chain, Turn Wheel Spindle as Indicated (All 1938-55 Models)

large hexagon-nut securing the bearing sleeve for the brake drum and chain-sprocket assembly. Slacken off the rear-brake adjuster. Then tighten the chain as required by screwing out *evenly* the two adjuster-screws in the rear-fork ends, after first loosening the lock-nuts. If you are in any doubt as to whether both adjuster screws have been turned the same amount, check the alignment of the front and rear wheels with a taut piece of string or with a straight-edge (see page 132). After making the necessary adjustment, tighten the adjuster screw lock-nuts. Before re-tightening the spindle nut on the off side, tighten the large hexagon-nut securing the brake-drum sleeve.

No Adjustment for Wheel Bearings. On all machines the hubs of both wheels have large-diameter journal-type ball bearings. These are non-adjustable and require no attention except oiling (see page 40) for many thousands of miles. Eventually if appreciable "shake" develops, renew the bearings.

To Adjust Front-fork Spindles (1938-46 Models). On machines with the Panther-Webb girder-type front forks, some slight side

GENERAL MAINTENANCE

play sometimes develops in the fork links, and this spoils good fork action and positive steering.

To take up side play, first slacken the front-fork shock-absorbers as much as possible, and then adjust each of the fork spindles in turn. Adjustment is correct when the small knurled washers are *free to rotate without any side play*. To take up side play on a spindle, loosen the lock-nuts at both ends, rotate the spindle *anti-clockwise a quarter of a turn*, firmly tighten the lock-nut on the near side, and then tighten the lock-nut on the off side. After dealing with each fork spindle, test the movement of the forks to make sure that the knurled washers are free (without end float), and that the spindle and links are not binding.

The Panther-Dowty "Oleomatic" and Panther forks fitted to 1947 and later models need no adjustment other than an occasional steering-head adjustment. For maintenance instructions see pages 116–18.

Play in Steering Head. During running-in the ball head-races in the frame and on the fork crown settle to a small extent. To detect any bearing play, apply the front brake, and with both wheels on the ground rock the machine to and fro. While doing this feel any play by placing a finger over the joint of the ball head-lug.

To Adjust Steering Head (1938-46 Models). If there is a little backlash in the front-brake anchor arm, allow for this when adjusting the steering-head bearing. To rectify slackness in the steering head, loosen the cotter nut on the near side of the ball head, punch back the cotter slightly, and then screw down as required the large head nut which forms the base of the steering-head damper. Turn the head nut only a fraction of a turn at a time. It is essential not to over-tighten it, otherwise the Panther will become unstable.

To Adjust Steering Head (1947 Onwards). With telescopic front-forks, loosen the two clamping bolts on the fork-crown fitting (see Fig. 18), and the pad bolt located on the handlebar clip lug. Then adjust the steering-head nut as required until the front forks are quite free to turn, but with no up-and-down movement in the head. After making the necessary adjustment, retighten firmly the pad bolt and the two clamping bolts.

Burman Clutch Adjustment. From a glance at Fig. 57 it will be apparent that wear of the Klingerite or cork inserts in the friction plates (and bedding down during running-in) gradually causes the clutch plates to close up towards each other, with the

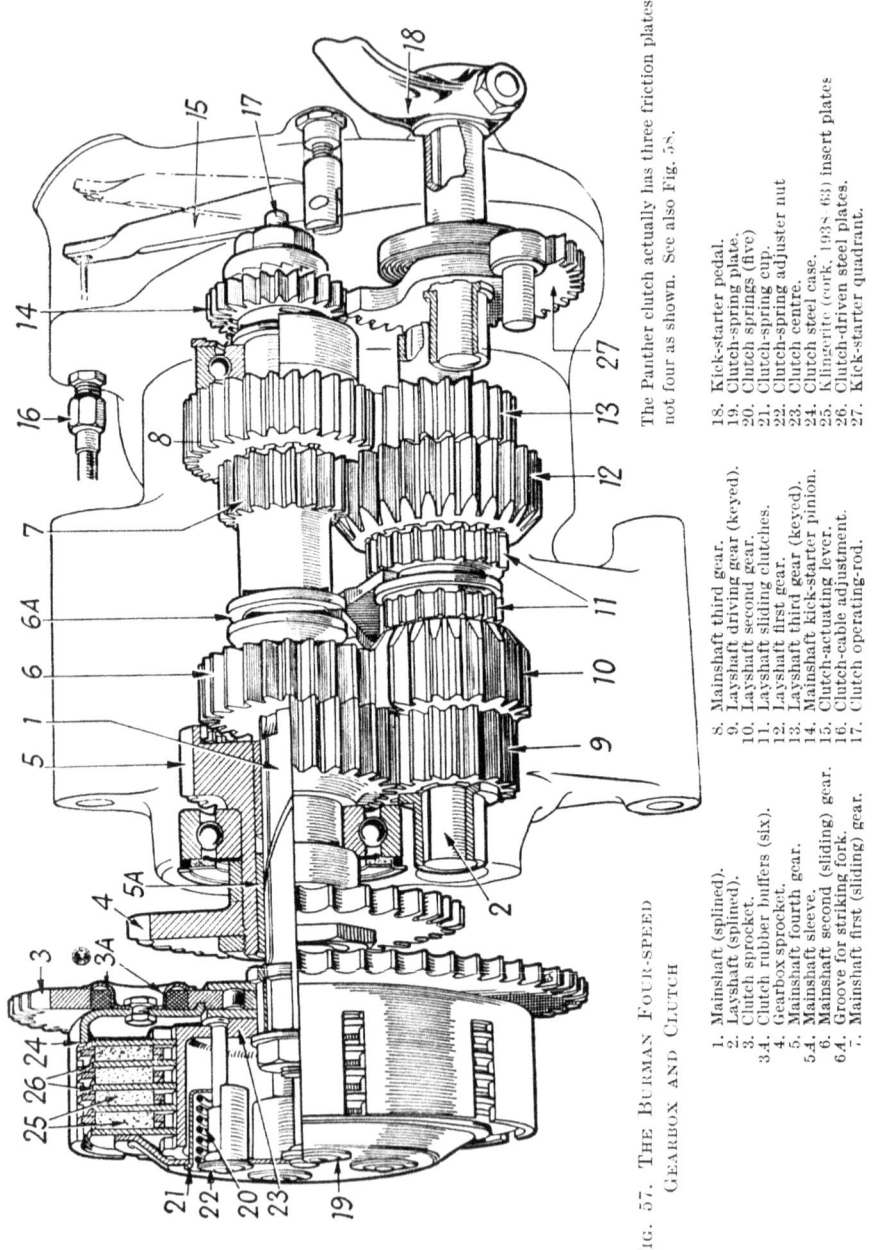

FIG. 57. THE BURMAN FOUR-SPEED GEARBOX AND CLUTCH

1. Mainshaft (splined).
2. Layshaft (splined).
3. Clutch sprocket.
3A. Clutch rubber buffers (six).
4. Gearbox sprocket.
5. Mainshaft fourth gear.
5A. Mainshaft sleeve.
6. Mainshaft second (sliding) gear.
6A. Groove for striking fork.
7. Mainshaft first (sliding) gear.
8. Mainshaft third gear.
9. Layshaft driving gear (keyed).
10. Layshaft second gear.
11. Layshaft sliding clutches.
12. Layshaft first gear.
13. Layshaft third gear (keyed).
14. Mainshaft kick-starter pinion.
15. Clutch-actuating lever.
16. Clutch-cable adjustment.
17. Clutch operating-rod.
18. Kick-starter pedal.
19. Clutch-spring plate.
20. Clutch springs (five).
21. Clutch-spring cup.
22. Clutch-spring adjuster nut.
23. Clutch centre.
24. Clutch steel case.
25. Klingerite (cork, 1938-63) insert plates
26. Clutch-driven steel plates.
27. Kick-starter quadrant.

The Panther clutch actually has three friction plates, not four as shown. See also Fig. 58.

NOTE: Detailed overhaul, adjustment and maintenance information for Burman gearboxes and clutches can be found in our publication - ISBN 9781588501813 result that the effective length of the clutch operating-rod (inside the hollow gearbox mainshaft) is increased. The clutch cable, however, tends to stretch with repeated use of the clutch lever and thereby to some extent neutralizes the effect of clutch-insert wear.

Clutch slip must be avoided at all costs, as it causes damage and over-heating, and spoils performance. Sometimes it is due to incorrect adjustment of the clutch springs (see page 126), but generally it is due to insufficient free movement in the clutch operating mechanism. Referring to Fig. 58, there must always be about $\frac{1}{32}$ in. clearance (with the clutch plates engaged) between the short clutch-operating plunger (B) and the nose of the operating lever (C). Periodically inspect and, if necessary, rectify the adjustment. Feel the approximate amount of free movement in the clutch control by noting when resistance is met with as the handlebar lever is operated. Klingerite type inserts swell when hot. Therefore make the required adjustment with the clutch cold. First make sure that the clutch cable is free in its casing.

1. **Effecting Minor Adjustment.** When wear of the friction inserts is such that only a minor adjustment is called for, loosen the locking nut on the cable adjuster, which is screwed into the rear of the kick-starter housing (see Fig. 57). Then unscrew, or screw up, a few turns the cable adjuster, according to whether it is desired to decrease or increase the effective length of the control cable respectively. Decreasing the effective length of the cable does, of course, reduce the clearance (see Fig. 58) between the operating plunger (B) and the nose of the operating lever (C). After making the required adjustment, retighten the locking nut on the cable adjuster.

2. **Effecting Major Adjustment.** If wear of the friction inserts is such that it is impossible to obtain correct adjustment of the clutch by a minor (cable) adjustment, a major adjustment is called for.

Referring to Fig. 58, to effect a major adjustment, first remove the two screws (H) with a suitable screwdriver, and detach the cap (G). Then proceed to adjust the sleeve nut (F) with an open-ended spanner until there is a clearance of about $\frac{1}{32}$ in. between the operating plunger (B) and the nose of the operating lever (C). To increase or decrease the clearance, turn the sleeve nut (F) clockwise or anti-clockwise respectively. Normally a sleeve nut adjustment of one or two turns is sufficient. Finally lock the sleeve nut by replacing the cap (G) and the two securing screws (H).

3. **Adjustment of Clutch Springs.** Clutch slip which persists with the operating mechanism and cable correctly adjusted may

occur because the springs require adjustment. Remove the outer half of the oil-bath chain case prior to an adjustment.

To make an adjustment, screw home *half a complete turn* each of the five spring adjuster-nuts (shown at 22 in Fig. 57). Then ascertain whether the clutch still slips. If it does, screw home a further half-turn each adjuster nut; be careful to adjust each nut exactly the same amount. Note that the five adjuster-nuts for

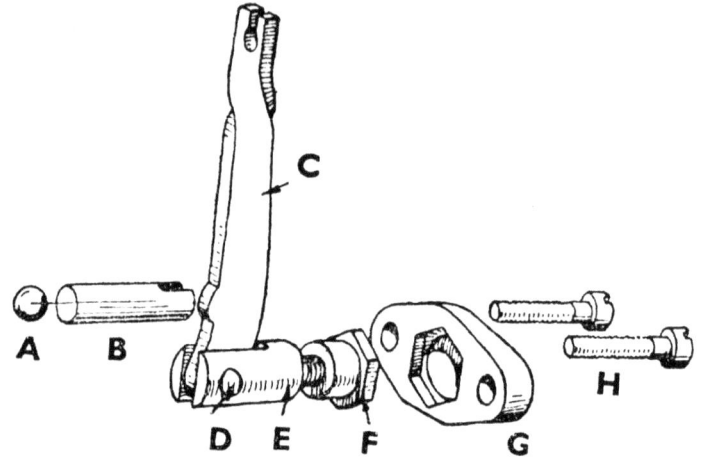

Fig. 58. Fulcrum Adjustment for the Clutch-operating Lever

For position in Burman gearbox, see Fig. 57.

A. Steel ball.
B. Short operating-plunger.
C. Operating lever.
D. Fulcrum pin.
E. Fork for operating lever.
F. Sleeve nut.
G. Cap for sleeve nut.
H. Cap-securing nut screws.

adjusting spring tension are correctly adjusted when their heads are *just flush with the outside of the clutch-spring plate*.

The most suitable tool for tightening the clutch spring adjuster-nuts is an old and broad screwdriver, slotted on the engaging edge.

If it is necessary to screw the five adjuster-nuts fully or almost home to prevent clutch slip, this indicates that the clutch springs have weakened and/or the Klingerite inserts are worn excessively and require to be renewed.

If the clutch does not free properly, the cause may be wear of the clutch-operating rod shown at 17 in Fig. 57. A minor clutch-cable adjustment should rectify matters.

To Remove Front Wheel (1938-46 Models). On machines with girder-type front forks, bring the front stand into use and disconnect the brake-cable yoke from the operating lever on the

GENERAL MAINTENANCE 127

brake drum anchor-plate. Also disconnect the speedometer drive at its lower end. Then loosen the front-wheel spindle nuts and lift the wheel out of the front forks, springing the fork blades slightly apart to assist wheel removal.

REPLACING. Replace the wheel in the reverse order of removal (as is given above). Be sure to reconnect the speedometer drive securely.

To Remove Front Wheel (1947-55). On machines with telescopic-type front forks first place some suitable packing beneath the crankcase to *fully extend* the front-fork legs and also raise the front wheel clear of the ground. Disconnect the brake cable from the brake-shoe operating lever.

Loosen *on the brake-drum side* the nuts holding the wheel-spindle securing cap. Unscrew the front-wheel spindle nut (on the same side) about *two complete turns*. Remove both spindle-securing caps and ease the front wheel out of the forks, supporting it as it comes clear of the fork legs.

REPLACING. Where "telescopics" are fitted, the procedure for replacing the front wheel is as follows. With suitable packing still supporting the crankcase, place the front-wheel assembly in position. Then tighten—*finger tight*—the four nuts securing the caps which retain the front wheel spindle (see Fig. 18). On *the brake-drum side* tighten the front-wheel spindle nut so that the wheel firmly contacts the side of the spindle fitting. Next tighten firmly the nuts securing the front-wheel spindle-retaining cap on the brake-drum side.

Raise the machine clear of the packing inserted below the crankcase, and "bounce" the front forks several times on the ground. Afterwards tighten the nuts securing the front wheel spindle-retaining cap on the near side. Finally reconnect and adjust the front-brake cable. The object of the "bouncing" is to see that the lower tubes of the fork legs slide freely in the outer tubes. A small clearance is provided for this purpose between the shoulder on the near-side spindle ferrule, and the spindle fitting.

To Remove Front Wheel (1956-7 Rigid-frame and 1957-62 Standard Spring-frame Model 100). Here a quickly-detachable front wheel with a "knock-out" spindle is fitted. It is desirable first to place some suitable packing beneath the engine crankcase so as to raise the front wheel well clear of the ground and steady the machine. Disconnect the brake operating-cable from the brake-shoe operating lever, on the off side. Next loosen the four nuts holding the wheel-spindle securing caps to the bottom ends of the telescopic fork-legs. Also remove the nut from the "knock-out" spindle; unscrew this spindle from the hub, tap it out, and withdraw the front wheel. Note carefully the order of the distance washers.

REPLACING. Replace the front wheel in the reverse order of removal. See that the distance washers are replaced in the correct order (as removed), and that the fork-end cap securing-nuts are firmly tightened. Make sure also that the "knock-out" spindle is firmly screwed home into the hub and that the spindle nut is spannered tightly.

To Remove Front Wheel (1956 Spring-frame, 1957-62 De Luxe Spring-frame Model 100, and 1959-66 Model 120). The front wheel has a full-width light-alloy hub and the wheel is interchangeable with the rear wheel. Both are mounted on $\frac{3}{4}$-in. diameter "knock-out" spindles.

Before removing the front wheel it is desirable to insert some packing beneath the crank-case. Disconnect the brake operating-cable from the brake-shoe operating lever on the off side by removing the clevis pin. Next slacken the clinch-bolt located at the bottom of the near-side fork leg and unscrew the nut on the off side of the hub spindle. Then withdraw the spindle, and the wheel will come adrift.

REPLACING. Proceed in the reverse order of removal. Be careful to retighten the hub-spindle nut firmly *before* retightening the clinch-bolt on the near side, otherwise the brake anchor-plate may not be properly located. Note that the brake operating-lever is secured to the cam spindle by fine serrations and thus has a wide range of adjustment.

To Remove Rear Wheel (1956 Spring-frame, 1957-62 Spring-frame De Luxe Model 100, and 1959-66 Model 120). As may be seen in Fig. 59, the quickly-detachable rear wheel comprises a combined brake drum and chain sprocket, the rear wheel proper, dust covers, and several distance collars; all are mounted on a $\frac{3}{4}$-in. diameter "knock-out" spindle.

To remove rear wheel, jack the machine up on its centre stand, unscrew the spindle nut (located on the off side), push the spindle through the assembly and remove the distance collars as they become free. It will be found that the aluminium end-plate has a tendency to remain in position, even when the spindle is withdrawn; this is because the inner boss on the end-plate runs inside an oil-seal lip; by inserting a finger inside the spindle hole you can pull the plate free. Then pull the rear wheel off the cush-drive studs, and allow it to fall away. By tilting the wheel slightly to one side, it can readily be removed from beneath the mudguard and the rear forks.

GENERAL MAINTENANCE

REPLACING. To replace the quickly-detachable rear wheel, reverse the withdrawal procedure. It will be found that if the rear wheel spindle is introduced through the fork lug into the hub it will be much easier to locate the driving studs into their respective holes in the hub. The outer spacing collar is shouldered to locate

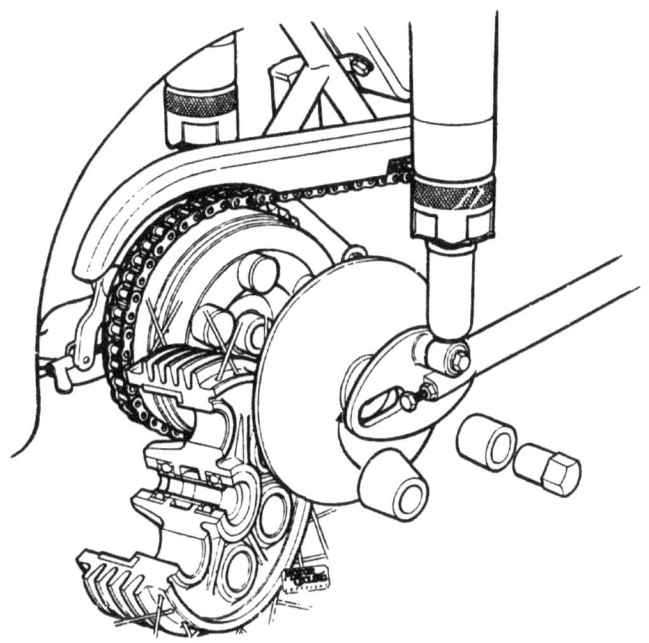

FIG. 59. SHOWING DETAILS OF 1956-66 QUICKLY-DETACHABLE REAR WHEEL WITH FULL-WIDTH LIGHT-ALLOY HUB
(*By courtesy of "Motor Cycling."*)

it in the slot in the rear-fork lug. Before tightening the spindle nut, make absolutely certain that the shoulders on this distance collar are properly fitted into the slot.

Removing Brake-drum Unit (Full-width Rear Hubs). You can, if you wish, remove the brake drum and chain-sprocket unit from the rear forks by disconnecting the secondary chain, and removing the large hexagon sleeved fixing-nut which clamps the unit to the rear-fork end. Access to the brake shoes is obtained by removing the brake plate through the sleeve on which it is located. Observe that the sleeve has a Woodruff key fitted which lines up with the key-way in the brake plate. When replacing the brake plate, be sure that the key is not displaced; its purpose is to prevent the centre sleeve from rotating when the large hexagon fixing-nut is being tightened down. Note that the speedometer-driving gears are inside the rear-brake casing. *Smear these with heavy grease once a season.* Note also that the rear-brake shoes have two "pull off" springs, while the front brake shoes have only one.

To Remove Rear Wheel (1938-55). The rear portion of the mudguard is hinged (rigids). Disconnect the tail-piece stays and lift the tail-piece up. Unscrew the wing nut from the rear-brake rod and also disconnect the secondary chain. On 1947 and later models disconnect the speedometer-drive cable from the speedometer gearbox. Loosen both rear-wheel spindle nuts and then carefully withdraw the rear wheel from the fork ends. It may be necessary to tilt the wheel sideways to disengage the brake anchor-plate from the locating stud.

REPLACING. Replace the rear wheel in the reverse order of dismantling. Before replacing it, see that the two cams (1938-55) are in line and firmly on the wheel-spindle flats. You need not bother about rear-wheel alignment being correct if the cams are kept hard up against the pegs in the frame (see Fig. 56).

See that you fit the spring link correctly (see page 120) on the secondary chain; on a 1947 or later model with rear-hub speedometer drive, do not forget to reconnect the drive firmly. Before tightening the rear-wheel spindle nuts firmly, adjust the secondary chain tension (see page 120) if necessary.

To Remove Rear Wheel (1956-7 Rigid-frame, 1957-62 Standard Model 100). Proceed in accordance with the preceding instructions for removing the rear wheel on 1938-55 models.

Notes on Lubricating Brakes and Hubs. The following should be noted in addition to the advice given on pages 40 and 42.

The grease nipple located in the centre of the boss carrying the brake cam operating-lever (front and rear on full-width hubs) conveys grease to the brake-cam spindle bush. Adequate lubrication is essential, but it is also important to avoid injecting excessive grease, otherwise some may penetrate to the brake-shoe linings and impair their efficiency.

On 1956-66 "springers" with full-width light-alloy hubs a grease nipple is located *inside* the front and rear hub. This nipple is accessible only when the wheel is removed. The nipple supplies grease to the large reservoir situated between the main bearings of the wheel. Normally it is sufficient to charge the reservoir with grease about every 5,000 miles. Note that the excessive injection of grease may force grease through the journals into the lubrication-seal cavities. Indeed, if gross over-lubrication is effected, the internal pressure of grease in the reservoir combined

GENERAL MAINTENANCE

with the rotation of the wheels may well cause actual bursting of the synthetic-rubber members in the lubrication seals.

Note that there is enough grease packed in the brake drum and sprocket assembly (full-width hubs) to suffice for thousands of miles. Do not therefore disturb the ball journal except when a complete overhaul is needed or when journal renewal is called for.

To Check Wheel Alignment (Sidecar Outfit). Two plain boards (about 6 ft. long, 3 to 4 in. wide, and about 1 in. thick) are needed. Each board must have one edge true. A third board similar, but about 4 ft. long, is also required.

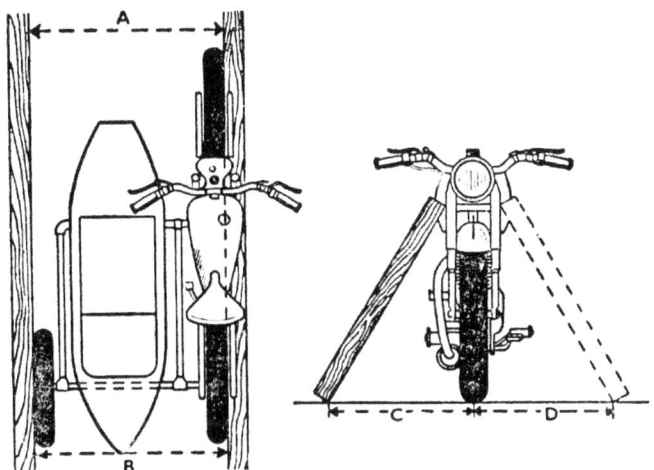

FIG. 60. CHECKING WHEEL ALIGNMENT ON SIDECAR OUTFIT

The motor-cycle wheels on 1938-55 models cannot get out of alignment except through an accident to the frame or forks, because the cam adjusters are fixed to the rear-wheel spindle for secondary-chain adjustment.

With correct alignment the motor-cycle and sidecar wheels must not be dead parallel, as this causes a tendency for the sidecar outfit to pull towards the near side. Some "toe-in" is essential.

To check the wheel alignment, first see that the outfit is on a level surface. Next place one of the long boards alongside the front and rear tyres of the motor-cycle so that it contacts the front and rear of the rear tyre. Then without disturbing this board, place the second board so that its true edge contacts the front and rear of the sidecar tyre as shown in Fig. 60.

Referring to Fig. 60, with a steel measuring-tape, check the dimensions A and B. To ensure the sidecar having the correct "toe-in," dimension *A* should measure approximately ½ in. less than dimension *B*.

After verifying wheel alignment, check that the motor-cycle itself is in correct vertical alignment. The sidecar chassis fittings on a new outfit sometimes take a permanent "set," causing the motor-cycle to become quite vertical or to lean slightly towards the sidecar. Neither is desirable.

Referring to Fig. 60 (right-hand illustration), take the wooden 4 ft. long board and rest it against a fixed point (at handlebar clinch-bolt height) on the upper part of the front forks. Mark the floor where the edge of the board contacts it. Then rest the board on the other side of the forks with the upper end of the board in precisely the corresponding position, and again mark the floor where the lower edge of the board touches it.

With a steel measuring-tape, check dimensions *C* and *D*. These two dimensions should not be equal if the machine is in correct alignment. The motor-cycle should lean *outwards* about ½ in., measured at handlebar clinch-bolt height.

To Check Wheel Alignment (Solo Model). In order to obtain maximum tyre life and good steering, it is essential always to keep the front and rear wheels in true alignment. Sometimes a severe crash will upset the alignment through slight distortion of the frame or front forks, and this type of mis-alignment can seldom be rectified except by the makers. Moving the rear wheel backwards in order to take up slackness in the secondary chain should not upset the wheel alignment, except perhaps on 1956-66 spring-frame models which have adjuster screws (see page 122) instead of a twin-cam adjustment of the wheel spindle; these cams give automatic alignment, so long as the adjusting cams (see Fig. 56) are kept hard up against the pegs fixed in the frame.

A rough check on wheel alignment can be made by kneeling behind the machine and taking a "sight" along the two wheels. It is preferable, however, to check the alignment by placing a straight-edge or board alongside the two wheels, or by using a taut piece of string attached to an anchorage post. The straight-edge or string should, of course, touch the front and rear tyres at four points (assuming both tyres are of the same size). Should there be any appreciable error in the alignment, rectify this by means of the chain adjusters in the rear fork-ends, and afterwards re-check the tension of the secondary chain (see page 120).

Transmission Shock-absorbers (1938-55 Model 100). As may be seen in Fig. 61, the chain wheel has on its inner side three metal vanes equally spaced round its boss. Between these vanes and three similar vanes in the hub are six rubber blocks. Thus there is, alternately, a metal vane and a rubber block.

GENERAL MAINTENANCE

About every 10,000 miles remove the chain-wheel and inspect the condition of the six rubber blocks. If these are distorted or damaged, renew them immediately. Lay the wheel on its side, fit the six rubber blocks, and before positioning the sprocket, smear some soft soap on the vanes. Also apply a film of grease to the bearing. This procedure will enable the sprocket to be pushed down readily prior to its final tightening.

In addition to the cush-hub shock-absorber, the drive from the

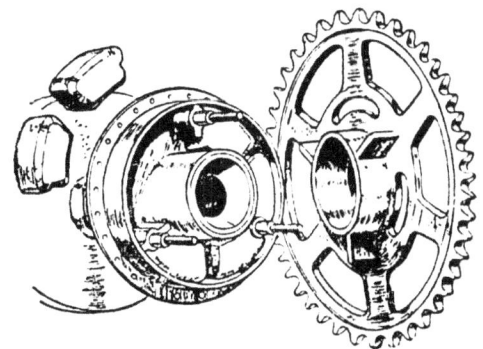

FIG. 61. DETAILS OF THE PANTHER CUSH-HUB SHOCK-ABSORBER

On all Panther models without full-width hubs.

clutch sprocket is transmitted to the clutch through six rubber buffers (one of which is shown at 3A in Fig. 57) which allow a radial movement of about $\frac{3}{16}$ in. Normally these rubber buffers do not require to be renewed until after a large mileage.

Transmission Shock-absorbers (1956-7 Full-width Hubs). The quickly-detachable rear wheel (see Fig. 59) is carried on six cush-drive studs which are evenly spaced on the off side of the rear-brake drum and sprocket unit. These cush-drive studs comprise inner and outer sleeves bonded together by rubber. They require no attention other than the smearing of a light film of oil on their outer driving surfaces each time the rear wheel is removed (see page 128).

The Spring-frame Shock-absorbers (1954-5). On 1954 and 1955 "springers" the spring frame is of the "swinging arm" type and includes two Armstrong designed telescopic-leg shock-absorbers with oil-damping. The Armstrong shock-absorbers normally require no topping up or other attention, but they are adjustable for load. All new Model 100 Panthers were delivered by the makers to Panther dealers with the suspension units adjusted for *solo* riding (except where a machine was bought with a sidecar attached), and a loading adjustment of the telescopic legs is called for when a pillion passenger and/or heavy luggage is

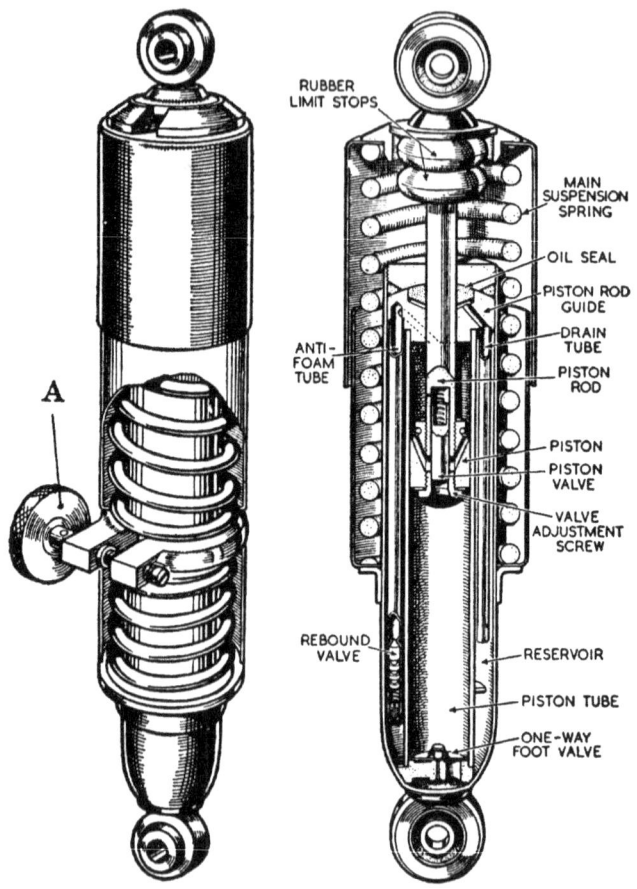

Fig. 62. Cut-away View (left) of 1954-5 Armstrong Two-rate Shock-absorber Unit, and (right) Sectioned View of 1956-66 Armstrong Shock-Absorber Unit
Note the knurled adjuster-screw *A* for varying the spring rate.

carried, or when a sidecar is fitted after purchase. The adjustment of the Armstrong shock-absorber units can be effected very quickly and simply.

Details of the Amstrong shock-absorber unit (1954-5 type) are shown in Fig. 62. At a point about $2\frac{1}{2}$ in. above the bottom of the lower internal suspension spring (see left-hand cut-away view) is an annular groove into which is clamped a split clamping-ring.

GENERAL MAINTENANCE 135

by a knurled adjusting screw *A*. With this screw tightened up and the clamping ring in the position illustrated in Fig. 62 the compression of the shock-absorber unit is resisted by the hydraulic-damper piston-valve and the main (top) suspension spring only; this spring requires a loading of 100 lb. to compress it one inch (i.e. the rate of the top spring is 100 lb. per in.). This setting (adjuster-screw tightened) is the one normally suitable for *pillion or sidecar work*.

To soften the rear suspension for *solo* riding (one up) it is only

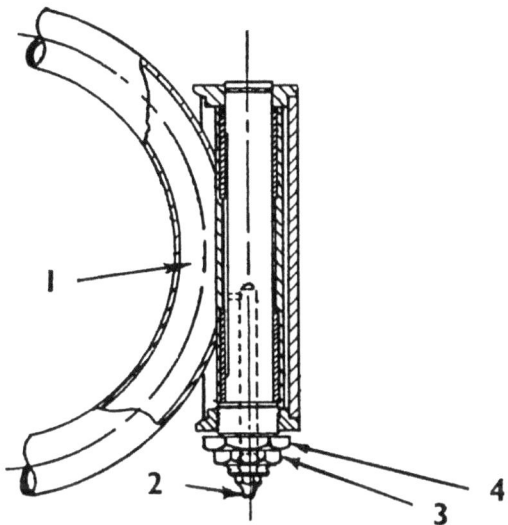

FIG. 63. THE "SWINGING ARM" PIVOT BEARING (1954-66).
1. Swinging arm. 3. Lock-nut for 4.
2. Grease nipple. 4. Bearing adjuster-nut.

necessary to unscrew the knurled adjuster-screw *A* and free the split clamping-ring from the annular groove; this allows the clamping ring to float up and down and bring *both* compression springs into action, thereby reducing the single-spring rate from 100 lb. per in. to a combined-spring rate of 71 lb. per in. Alternative springs are available to give combined-spring rates of 130 lb. per in. (two up) and 100 lb. per in. (solo).

If you wish to change over from solo riding to passenger carrying, you can easily re-set the clamping ring in the annular groove and tighten the adjuster screw. With the suspension unit adjusted for solo riding, the total up-and-down movement of the clamping ring is only about ¾ in., and its fixed position can therefore readily be obtained.

Note that as the clamping ring floats between the two springs (when riding solo), frictional wear of the clamping ring is negligible and no lubrication is necessary. All new springs are greased when assembled, and this grease suffices for an indefinite period.

The Spring-frame Shock-absorbers (1956-66). On 1956-66 "swinging arm" Models 100 and 120 rear suspension shock-absorber units of improved design are provided. The internal details are shown in Fig. 62 (*right*). Like the 1954-5 units, these require no topping-up or other attention, but they are readily adjustable for load. If the machine has a sidecar attached, and a heavy pillion passenger is carried, it is desirable to adjust each unit so that the lobe of its adjusting sleeve rests in the cup provided at the bottom of the unit. Machines are normally delivered to Panther dealers with the rear-suspension units adjusted to give maximum shock-absorber movement (the usual adjustment for solo riding).

The "Swinging Arm" (1954 "Springers" Onwards). It is advisable to lubricate the "swinging arm" pivot bearing about every 500 miles (see page 43). It is also desirable very occasionally to take up any end-play which may develop in the "swinging arm" pivot bearing.

Referring to Fig. 63, to take up end-play in the pivot bearing, hold the bearing adjuster-nut (4) with one spanner, and with another spanner loosen the lock-nut (3) by turning it *anti-clockwise one half-turn*. Now turn the adjuster nut (4) *clockwise* until no perceptible end-play can be felt in the pivot bearing. Afterwards re-tighten the lock-nut (3). When doing this, hold the adjuster nut (4) with a spanner to prevent its turning and upsetting the bearing adjustment. Then again check the "swinging arm" bearing for end-play. It is important to avoid locking the bearing solid; to ensure that this has not been done, "bounce" the rear of the motor-cycle and see that no undue resistance is offered to the normal telescopic action of the Armstrong shock-absorbers.

INDEX

AIR—
  filters, 112-13
  leakage, front fork, 118
  release valve, 34
Alignment—
  headlamp, 66
  wheel, 131-2
Amal carburettor, 17-26, 108-112
Automatic ignition-timing unit, 36, 53, 54

BARREL, cylinder, removing, 90
Battery, 62-6
Brakes, 11
  adjustment, 118
  lubricating, 42, 130
Brushes, commutator, 58
Bulb renewal, 72

CABLE, pick-up, renewing, 52
Cam—
  adjustment, rear wheel, 120, 130, 132
  followers, removing, 107
Carbon deposits, 45, 84, 96
Carburettor, 17-26, 108-112
  assembly, 26, 112
  dismantling, 25, 109
  flange, checking, 88, 112
  removing, 87, 109
  settings, 22, 109
  tuning, 22-5, 109
Chain tension, 60, 119
Chromium, cleaning, 116
Circlips, 91, 100
Clutch, 9, 123
  shock absorber, 133
Commutator, 58
Compensated-voltage-control, 60
Compression rings, 93-6
Connecting-rod bearings, 98
Consumption, fuel and oil, 16, 24
Contact-breaker maintenance, 35, 51
Controls, 4
Cornering with sidecar, 13

Crankcase—
  draining, 33
  pressure in, 34
Cut-out, 60
Cylinder—
  barrel, 90, 100
  base washer, 101
  examining, 94
  head, 88
  cleaning, 102

DAMPER, steering, 14
Decarbonizing, 84-105
Decompressor, 5, 107
Dimming-switch lubrication, 42
Dip-stick, 32
Draining—
  gearbox, 38
  sump, 33
Dynamo—
  chain, 37, 60
  drive, 55
  leads, 74
  lubrication, 34-7
  maintenance, 58-62
  output, 61
"Dyno-mag," 35, 51

ELECTRICAL controls, 5, 66
Enamel, cleaning, 116
Engine—
  cleaning, 82
  controls, 4, 6
  lubrication, 27-37
  maintenance, items for, 79
  number, 1
  oil, 32
  overhaul, complete, 108
  removing from frame, 108, 104
Exhaust—
  condition of, 21
  pipes, removing, 87
  valve lifter, 84, 88, 102

FILTERS, cleaning, 33, 104
Fins, cleaning, 82

Flame, exhaust, 21
Float chamber, inspecting, 25, 111
Flooding, causes of, 25
Footrest adjustment, 3
Fork spindles, 42, 122
Frame number, 1
Front—
  forks, 40-2, 116-18, 122
  stand, oiling, 43
  wheel, removing, 126-28
Fuel—
  consumption, 16, 24
  deposits, 45
  replenishment, 5
Fuse, absence of, 74

GAP—
  contact-breaker, 49-51
  piston ring, 93-6, 99
  plug, 47
Gasket, cylinder head, 89
Gauze filter, cleaning, 33, 104
Gear—
  change lever, 3, 9, 37
  changing, 9-11
  indicator, 9
Gearbox lubrication, 37-8
Gears, timing case, 105
Grease, 39
  gun, 39-40
Grinding-in valves, 97
Gudgeon-pin, 91, 100

HANDLEBAR, 3
  levers, lubricating, 42
Headlamp—
  focusing, 66-70
  position, adjusting, 66
  switch, 69, 77
High-tension pick-up, 52
Hill, negotiating, 12
Horn, electric, 73
Hub—
  bearings, 122, 130
  lubrication, 40, 130
Hydrometer, 64

IGNITION, 44-57
  lever, 6, 9
  timing, 53-7
  unit, automatic, 53-5

Indicator—
  gear, 9
  rod, 56
Intermediate gear, 29, 107

JET—
  block, inspecting, 26, 111
  main, 20, 22, 109
  pilot, 23-4, 109

KICK-STARTER lubrication, 37
Knocking, 16, 84

LAMPS, cleaning, 73
Lighting switch positions, 66
Linings, brake, 119
Loading indicator fork, 117
Lubrication points, 38

"MAGDYNO," 36, 50-3
Magneto, 34, 35, 50-4
Main jet, 20, 22, 109
"Monobloc" carburettor, 108-112

NEEDLE—
  jet, 20, 24, 26, 111
  valve, chain-case, 38
"Neutral," 11
"Nife" battery, 61

OIL, 5, 32
  bath, replenishing, 38
  circulation, 27-9, 31
  consumption, 16, 31
  control ring, 95, 99
  ducts, cylinder head, 99
  pressure, 31
  pump, 29
Oiled-up plug, 45
Overhead valve gear lubrication, 34
Over-rich mixture, 7, 33, 24

PETROL—
  consumption, 16, 24
  pipe unions, tightening, 103
  tank, 86, 103
  taps, 5
Pick-up, h.t., 52
Pilot—
  air screw, 20, 23, 109
  bulb, 71

INDEX

Pilot (contd.)—
  jet, 23-4, 109
Piston—
  examining, 94
  removing, 91
  replacing, 100
  rings, 93-6, 99
  seizure, 94
Pitted contacts, 51
Pitting, valve and seat, 97
Play, steering head, 123
Plug, sparking, 44-9
Polishing valve stems, 97
"Pre-focused" bulb, 71
Pressure gauge, tyre, 115
Primary chain, 38, 119
Pump, oil, 29

REAR—
  lamp, 71
  stand, 7, 43
  suspension, 43, 133-6
  wheel, removing, 128-30
Rebore, 95
Reflector, cleaning, 73
Repairs, 79
Reserve fuel supply, 5, 14
Ring, piston, 93-6, 99
Rotor, pump, 30
Running-in, 18, 45, 82

SECONDARY chain, 38, 120
Shock absorbers, 132-6
Shoes, brake, 119
Sidecar—
  alignment, 14, 131
  driving, 12
  forks, inflating, 117
  lamp bulb, 72
  lubrication, 40
  tyre pressures, 115
Silencer removal, 87, 97
Slip-ring, 52
Slow-running adjustment, 23, 109
Smeared lands, 94
Sparking plugs, 44-9
Speedometer, 2, 42, 130
Spitting-back, 23, 109
Split collets, 89, 99
Spring—
  clutch, adjusting, 125
  commutator brush, 58

Spring (contd.)—
  frame, 43, 133-6
  valve, 89, 98
Starting, 5-8
Steering, 12
  damper, 14
  head adjustment, 123
Stopping, 12
Switch, lighting, 66

TANK, removing, 86
Taper needle, 20, 24
Tappet adjustment, 82
Taps, petrol, 5
Telescopic front-forks, 116-18, 122
Terminals, battery, 64
Third-brush control, 61
Throttle—
  stop screw, 19, 23, 109
  valve, 20, 23, 26, 111, 112
Timing—
  control, automatic, 36
  cover, replacing, 107
  gears, 105-8
  ignition, 53-7
Tools, 79, 83
Top-dead-centre, 55
Topping-up—
  battery, 62
  front forks, 40
Transmission shock absorbers, 132
Tyres, 115

VALVE—
  clearances, 82
  cores, tyre, 115
  grinding, 97
  guides, 98
  holder, 81
  lift, 105
  ports, decarbonizing, 96
  seals, testing, 99
  springs, 98
    compressor, 81, 89
  timing, 105

WEAK mixture, 21, 23
Wheel—
  alignment, 131-2
  bearings, 120, 130
  removal, 126-30
Wiring, 74

AUTOBOOKS WORKSHOP MANUALS

ALFA ROMEO GIULIA 1300, 1600, 1750, 2000 1962-1978 WSM
BMW 1600 1966-1973 WSM
BMW 2500, 2800, 3.0 & 3.3 1968-1977 WSM
BMW 316, 320, 320i 1975-1977 WSM
BMW 518, 520, 520i 1973-1981 WSM
FIAT 1100, 1100D, 1100R & 1200 1957-1969 WSM
FIAT 124 1966-1974 WSM
FIAT 124 SPORT 1966-1975 WSM
FIAT 125 & 125 SPECIAL 1967-1973 WSM
FIAT 126, 126L, 126 DV, 126/650 & 126/650 DV 1972-1982 WSM
FIAT 127 SALOON, SPECIAL & SPORT, 900, 1050 1971-1981 WSM
FIAT 128 1969-1982 WSM
FIAT 1300, 1500 1961-1967 WSM
FIAT 131 MIRAFIORI 1975-1982 WSM
FIAT 132 1972-1982 WSM
FIAT 500 1957-1973 WSM
FIAT 600, 600D & MULTIPLA 1955-1969 WSM
FIAT 850 1964-1972 WSM
JAGUAR MK 1, 2 1955-1969 WSM
JAGUAR S TYPE, 420 1963-1968 WSM
JAGUAR XK 120, 140, 150 MK 7, 8, 9 1948-1961 WSM
LAND ROVER 1, 2 1948-1961 WSM
MERCEDES-BENZ 190 1959-1968 WSM
MERCEDES-BENZ 220/8 1968-1972 WSM
MERCEDES-BENZ 220B 1959-1965 WSM
MERCEDES-BENZ 230 1963-1968 WSM
MERCEDES-BENZ 250 1968-1972 WSM
MERCEDES-BENZ 280 1968-1972 WSM
MINI 1959-1980 WSM
MORRIS MINOR 1952-1971 WSM
PEUGEOT 404 1960-1975 WSM
PORSCHE 911 1964-1973 WSM
PORSCHE 911 1970-1977 WSM
RENAULT 16 1965-1979 WSM
RENAULT 8, 10, 1100 1962-1971 WSM
ROVER 3500, 3500S 1968-1976 WSM
SUNBEAM RAPIER, ALPINE 1955-1965 WSM
TRIUMPH SPITFIRE, GT6, VITESSE 1962-1968 WSM
TRIUMPH TR4, TR4A 1961-1967 WSM
VOLKSWAGEN BEETLE 1968-1977 WSM

VELOCEPRESS AUTOMOBILE BOOKS & MANUALS

ABARTH BUYERS GUIDE
AUSTIN-HEALEY 6-CYLINDER WSM
AUSTIN-HEALEY SPRITE & MG MIDGET 1958-1971 WSM
BMW 600 LIMOUSINE FACTORY WSM
BMW 600 LIMOUSINE OWNERS HAND BOOK & SERVICE MANUAL
BMW 2000 & 2002 1966-1976 WSM
BMW ISETTA FACTORY WSM
CARRERA PANAMERICANA - MEXICAN ROAD RACE (BOOK OF)
COMPLETE CATALOG OF JAPANESE MOTOR VEHICLES
CORVAIR 1960-1969 OWNERS WORKSHOP MANUAL
CORVETTE V8 1955-1962 OWNERS WORKSHOP MANUAL
DIALED IN - THE JAN OPPERMAN STORY
FERRARI 250/GT SERVICE AND MAINTENANCE
FERRARI 308 SERIES BUYER'S AND OWNER'S GUIDE
FERRARI BERLINETTA LUSSO
FERRARI BROCHURES AND SALES LITERATURE 1946-1967
FERRARI BROCHURES AND SALES LITERATURE 1968-1989
FERRARI GUIDE TO PERFORMANCE
FERRARI OPP, MAINTENANCE & SERVICE H/BOOKS 1948-1963
FERRARI OWNER'S HANDBOOK
FERRARI SERIAL NUMBERS PART I - ODD NUMBERS TO 21399
FERRARI SERIAL NUMBERS PART II - EVEN NUMBERS TO 1050
FERRARI SPYDER CALIFORNIA
FERRARI TUNING TIPS & MAINTENANCE TECHNIQUES
HENRY'S FABULOUS MODEL "A" FORD
HOW TO BUILD A FIBERGLASS CAR
HOW TO BUILD A RACING CAR
HOW TO RESTORE THE MODEL 'A' FORD
IF HEMINGWAY HAD WRITTEN A RACING NOVEL
JAGUAR E-TYPE 3.8 & 4.2 WSM
LE MANS 24 (THE BOOK THAT THE FILM WAS BASED ON)
MASERATI BROCHURES AND SALES LITERATURE
MASERATI OWNER'S HANDBOOK
METROPOLITAN FACTORY WSM
MGA & MGB OWNERS HANDBOOK & WSM
MG MIDGET TC, TD, TF & TF1500 WORKSHOP MANUAL
OBERT'S FIAT GUIDE
PERFORMANCE TUNING THE SUNBEAM TIGER
PORSCHE 356 1948-1965 WSM
PORSCHE 912 WSM
SOUPING THE VOLKSWAGEN
SOLEX CARBURETORS (EMPHASIS ON UK & EU AUTOMOBILES)
SU CARBURETORS (EMPHASIS ON UK AUTOMOBILES)
TRIUMPH TR2, TR3, TR4 1953-1965 WSM
TUNING FOR SPEED (P.E. IRVING)
VEDA ORR'S NEW REVISED HOT ROD PICTORIAL
VOLKSWAGEN TRANSPORTER, TRUCKS, STATION WAGONS WSM
VOLVO 1944-1968 ALL MODELS WSM
WEBER CARBURETORS (EMPHASIS ON ALFA & FIAT)

VELOCEPRESS THREE WHEELER BOOKS & MANUALS

BSA THREE WHEELER (BOOK OF)

BROOKLANDS BOOKS & ROAD TEST PORTFOLIOS (RTP)

AC CARS 1904-2009
ALFA ROMEO 1920-1933 ROAD TEST PORTFOLIO
ALFA ROMEO 1934-1940 ROAD TEST PORTFOLIO
BRABHAM RALT HONDA THE RON TAURANAC STORY
BUGATTI TYPE 10 TO TYPE 40 ROAD TEST PORTFOLIO
BUGATTI TYPE 10 TO TYPE 251 ROAD TEST PORTFOLIO
BUGATTI TYPE 41 TO TYPE 55 ROAD TEST PORTFOLIO
BUGATTI TYPE 57 TO TYPE 251 ROAD TEST PORTFOLIO
DELAHAYE ROAD TEST PORTFOLIO
FERRARI ROAD CARS 1946-1956 ROAD TEST PORTFOLIO
FIAT 500 1936-1972 ROAD TEST PORTFOLIO
FIAT DINO ROAD TEST PORTFOLIO
HISPANO SUIZA ROAD TEST PORTFOLIO
HONDA ST1100/ST1300 PAN EUROPEAN 1990-2002 RTP
JAGUAR MK1 & MK2 ROAD TEST PORTFOLIO
LOTUS CORTINA ROAD TEST PORTFOLIO
MV AGUSTA F4 750 & 1000 1997-2007 ROAD TEST PORTFOLIO
TATRA CARS ROAD TEST PORTFOLIO

VELOCEPRESS MOTORCYCLE BOOKS & MANUALS

1930'S BRITISH MOTORCYCLE CARBS & ELEC COMPONENTS (BOOK OF)
1930'S BRITISH MOTORCYCLE GEARBOXES & CLUTCHES (BOOK OF)
AJS SINGLES & TWINS 250cc THRU 1000cc 1932-1948 (BOOK OF)
AJS SINGLES 1955-65 350cc & 500cc (BOOK OF)
AJS SINGLES 1945-60 350cc & 500cc MODELS 16 & 18 (BOOK OF)
ARIEL 1939-1960 4 STROKE SINGLES (BOOK OF)
ARIEL LEADER & ARROW 1958-1964 (BOOK OF)
ARIEL MOTORCYCLES 1933-1951 WSM
ARIEL PREWAR MODELS 1932-1939 (BOOK OF)
BMW M/CYCLES R26 R27 (1956-1967) FACTORY WSM
BMW M/CYCLES R50 R50S R60 R69S (1955-1969) FACTORY WSM
BSA BANTAM ALL MODELS FROM 1948 ONWARDS (BOOK OF)
BSA SINGLES & V-TWINS UP TO 1927 (BOOK OF)
BSA SINGLES & V-TWINS UP TO 1935 (BOOK OF)
BSA SINGLES & V-TWINS 1936-1939 (BOOK OF)
BSA SINGLES & V-TWINS 1936-1952 (BOOK OF)
BSA SINGLES & V-TWINS 1936-1952 (BOOK OF)
BSA OHV & SV SINGLES 250-600cc 1945-1954 (BOOK OF)
BSA OHV & SV SINGLES - 250cc 1954-1970 (BOOK OF)
BSA OHV SINGLES 350 & 500cc 1955-1967 (BOOK OF)
BSA TWINS 1948-1962 (BOOK OF)
BSA TWINS 1962-1969 (SECOND BOOK OF)
CATALOG OF BRITISH MOTORCYCLES (1951 MODELS)
DOUGLAS PRE-WAR ALL MODELS 1929-1939 (BOOK OF)
DOUGLAS POST-WAR ALL MODELS 1948-1957 FACTORY WSM
DUCATI 160cc, 250cc & 350cc OHC MODELS FACTORY WSM
HONDA 50 ALL MODELS UP TO 1970 INC MONKEY & TRAIL (BOOK OF)
HONDA 90 ALL MODELS UP TO 1966 (BOOK OF)
HONDA MOTORCYCLES 125-150 TWINS C/CS/CB/CA WSM
HONDA MOTORCYCLES 200-305 TWINS C/CS/CB WSM
HONDA MOTORCYCLES C100 SUPER CUB WSM
HONDA MOTORCYCLES C110 SPORT CUB 1962-1969 WSM
HONDA TWINS & SINGLES 50cc THRU 305cc 1960-1966 (BOOK OF)
HONDA TWINS ALL MODELS 125cc THRU 450cc UP TO 1968 (BOOK OF)
INDIAN PONYBIKE, BOY RACER & PAPOOSE ILL PARTS LIST & SALES LIT
J.A.P. ENGINES 1927-1952 & MOTORCYCLES 1934-1952 (BOOK OF)
LAMBRETTA ALL 125 & 150cc MODELS 1947-1957 (BOOK OF)
LAMBRETTA LI & TV MODELS 1957-1970 (SECOND BOOK OF)
MATCHLESS 350 & 500cc SINGLES 1945-1956 (BOOK OF)
MATCHLESS 350 & 500cc SINGLES 1955-1966 (BOOK OF)
MOTORCYCLE ENGINEERING (P. E. Irving)
NORTON 1932-1947 (BOOK OF)
NORTON 1938-1956 (BOOK OF)
NORTON DOMINATOR TWINS 1955-1965 (BOOK OF)
NORTON MODELS 19, 50 & ES2 1955-1963 (BOOK OF)
NORTON MOTORCYCLES 1957-1970 FACTORY WSM
NORTON PREWAR MODELS 1932-1939 (BOOK OF)
NSU PRIMA ALL MODELS 1956-1964 (BOOK OF)
NSU QUICKLY ALL MODELS 1953-1963 (BOOK OF)
PANTHER HEAVYWEIGHT MOTORCYCLES 600 & 650cc (BOOK OF)
PANTHER LIGHTWEIGHT MOTORCYCLES 250 & 350cc (BOOK OF)
RALEIGH MOPEDS 1960-1969 (BOOK OF)
RALEIGH MOTORCYCLES 1919-1933 (BOOK OF)
ROYAL ENFIELD SINGLES & V TWINS 1934-1946 (BOOK OF)
ROYAL ENFIELD SINGLES & V TWINS 1937-1953 (BOOK OF)
ROYAL ENFIELD SINGLES 1946-1962 (BOOK OF)
ROYAL ENFIELD 736cc INTERCEPTOR FACTORY WSM
ROYAL ENFIELD 250cc & 350cc SINGLES 1958-1966 (SECOND BOOK OF)
RUDGE MOTORCYCLES 1933-1939 (BOOK OF)
SPEED AND HOW TO OBTAIN IT
SUNBEAM MOTORCYCLES 1928-1939 (BOOK OF)
SUNBEAM S7 & S8 1946-1957 (BOOK OF)
SUZUKI 50 & 80cc UP TO 1966 (BOOK OF)
SUZUKI T10 1963-1967 FACTORY WSM
SUZUKI T20 & T200 1965-1969 FACTORY WSM
TRIUMPH PRE-WAR MOTORCYCLE 1935-1939 (BOOK OF)
TRIUMPH MOTORCYCLES 1935-1949 (BOOK OF)
TRIUMPH MOTORCYCLES 1937-1951 WSM
TRIUMPH MOTORCYCLES 1945-1955 FACTORY WSM
TRIUMPH TWINS 1945-1958 (BOOK OF)
TRIUMPH TWINS 1956-1969 (BOOK OF)
VELOCETTE ALL SINGLES & TWINS 1925-1970 (BOOK OF)
VESPA 1951-1961 (BOOK OF)
VESPA 125 & 150cc & GS MODELS 1955-1963 (SECOND BOOK OF)
VESPA 90, 125 & 150cc 1963-1972 (THIRD BOOK OF)
VESPA GS & SS 1955-1968 (BOOK OF)
VILLIERS ENGINE UP TO 1959 INC. 3 WHEELERS (BOOK OF)
VILLIERS ENGINE UP TO 1969 (BOOK OF)
VINCENT MOTORCYCLES 1935-1955 WSM

FOR DETAILED DESCRIPTIONS PLEASE VISIT: www.VelocePress.com

www.ingramcontent.com/pod-product-compliance
Lightning Source LLC
Chambersburg PA
CBHW070552170426
43201CB00012B/1820